What They're Saying About Ruthie's Cookbooks...

"Ruthie's theme throughout her cookbooks is offering recipes which have just 3 ingredients, making cooking fast, easy and economical."

Sally Carroll
Weekly Vista, Bella Vista, AR

"With her 3 ingredient cookbook, Ruthie Wornall predicts you'll find cooking as easy as 1-2-3... It was her inexperience at cooking that paved the way to her success as the author of a series of 3 ingredient cookbooks."

Teresa Mattson
St. Joseph News Press,
St. Joseph, MO

"Her cookbooks are aimed at working women who don't have time to prepare fancy meals."

Anita French
The Morning News
Fayetteville, AR

"Ruthie Wornall mixes up 3 ingredient dishes and often speaks on the subject of 'How to Cook Dinner in 10 Minutes' and 'How to Throw A Party In 10 Minutes.'"

Jane Dunlap Christenson
Harrison Daily Times, Harrison, AR

"Ruthie Wornall has an easy Thanksgiving dinner menu that is also fast, tasty and somewhat economical, since each dish contains only 3 ingredients."

Mature Living Magazine,
November 1999

"Wornall's books are the result of her own search for easy recipes."

Iola, KS Newspaper

"Ruthie Wornall turned an idea for a Christmas gift into a series of cookbooks that call for only 3 ingredients."

Charles Feruzza
Overland Park Sun

"When cookbook author, Ruthie Wornall, enters the kitchen, less is more."

Shawnee News-Star

"One finds her to not only be a bit ornery, but also a strong business woman."

Shelly Davis
Woman's Edition Magazine

"If a recipe has more than 3 ingredients, it's not easy!"

Charles Feruzza
Overland Park Sun

THE BEST OF

★ ★ ★

COOKING

WITH

3

INGREDIENTS

Best of 3 Ingredients Cooking

1st Printing	May 2003
2nd Printing	July 2003
3rd Printing	September 2005
4th Printing	March 2006
5th Printing	April 2006
6th Printing	January 2007

ISBN 1-931294-11-9 - Hardcover
ISBN 1-931294-13-5 - Paperback

Library of Congress Number: 2001099917

Illustrated by Nancy Murphy Griffith

Edited, Designed and Published in the
United States of America
Manufactured in China
Cookbook Resources, LLC
541 Doubletree Drive
Highland Village, Texas 75077
Toll free 866-229-2665
www.cookbookresources.com

cookbook
resources LLC

In The Author's Words

I couldn't cook when I got married and I needed help. I started collecting 3-ingredient recipes that were so easy I couldn't ruin them. I tested them by cooking Christmas dinner for my husband's family and nobody knew I couldn't cook. I even fooled my mother-in-law. She proclaimed me a gourmet cook.

Since then I've parleyed not being able to cook into a series of 12, 3-Ingredient Cookbooks and have proved that quick, easy and even elegant recipes don't have to be complicated.

When I first decided to write and sell the books my husband said, 'You might sell 100.' Now that my sales are pushing 150,000 I take pleasure in reminding him that behind every successful woman there's a very surprised man.

In trying to help myself, I'm delighted to discover that I've helped other people, too. The books have been transcribed into Braille and used to teach cooking in schools for the blind, in hospice programs and in homes for the educable mentally disabled. They have been lifesavers for new brides, busy moms, college students, widowers, children learning to cook, retired people who want to cook the easy way, people with chronic fatigue syndrome, wheel chair chefs and for people with other disabilities.

I've made a career of helping busy people cook "Fast Food at Home". These books have shown them how to use convenience foods in unique ways to create memorable dishes for family and friends. Busy people do have time to cook when they can prepare dinner in minutes with these 3-ingredient recipes.

This book contains recipes in all categories ranging from appetizers and beverages, to soups, salads, vegetables, main dishes, breads and desserts which enable you to prepare entire dinners in minutes. It incorporates short-cuts into recipes which save time, but don't compromise taste.

When you use these quick and easy recipes you'll find cooking is fun and you won't mind preparing dinners and entertaining, because now it is EASY TO COOK.

Happy Cooking!

Ruthie Wornall

About the Author

Ruthie Wornall is a busy lady whose everyday life demands simplicity wherever she can find it. She's been happily married for 30 years, has two children and three grandchildren and resides in Kansas.

When she married, she could not cook and began collecting recipes with only 3 ingredients. Over the years, she's turned her collection of recipes into a series of 12 cookbooks, each with recipes containing only 3 ingredients.

Over the years, she has written food columns using her 3-ingredient recipes, has made TV and personal appearances across the Midwest and has preached simplicity wherever she goes.

Today she helps coordinate medical, mission trips to Guanajuato, Mexico, teaches Spanish, writes culinary, murder mysteries, dotes on her new twin grandchildren and continues to cook using only 3 ingredients in each recipe.

Contents

New Year's Eve Party

The diet doesn't start until next week so for now eat, drink and be merry. Here are recipes you can whip up and still enjoy the party.

Appetizers
for Saint Patrick's Day Party

St. Patrick was the patron of Ireland and a saint in the Roman Catholic Church. He began over 300 churches in Ireland and lived between 389 and 461. While corned beef and cabbage is the traditional fare on Saint Patrick's Day, any of the appetizers below would be great to take to a Saint Patrick's Day party.

A Valentine Dinner Menu

You don't have to spend forever in the kitchen preparing for a special occasion. This Valentine's Day Dinner is a sweetheart of a meal.

Cornish Hen A La Orange 154

Pecan-Rice Pilaf 116

Strawberry Souffle Salad 84

Green Beans Amandine 124

Cookie Kisses 217

Easy Dinner for New Brides

This dinner is so easy you can't ruin it, even if you've never cooked before!

Ernie Massey's Italian Chicken 141

Cranberry Apple Salad 80

Men's Favorite Green Beans 123

Clover Leaf Rolls 71

Chocolate Walnut Drops 223

You always want the best for family and friends and these 2 special dinners are all made just for them. With very little time and very little effort, you will be the most popular person there when you serve these meals.

Easy Sunday Dinner

Merle's Cornish Hen A La Orange 154
Long Grain Wild Rice Amandine 116
Snow Peas 127
Boston Bibb Lettuce Salad 91
Brickle Chip Brownies 224

Quick 'N Easy Cookin'

Rosebillie Horn's Old Fashioned Roast Beef 158
Rosemary Roasted Potatoes 109
Green Beans Amandine 124
Romaine-Melon Salad 90
Frozen Lemonade Pie 232

Easy Menu Ideas

Even gourmet cooks need a break every now and then and this Quick Gourmet Dinner and Easy Pork Tenderloin Dinner are great escapes, look good and taste good and no one will know there are just 3 ingredients in every recipe.

Quick Gourmet Dinner

Easy Pork Tenderloin Dinner

Easy Menu Ideas

100-Years-Old and Still Cooking!

My Grandma Davis is over 100-years-old and she's still cooking, taking care of her 4-bedroom house, gardening, quilting and has written two books of poetry while in her nineties. These are two of her favorite menus.

Mother's Pot Roast

Easy Pot Roast Dinner

These turkey and chicken dinners come without the wear and tear on your nerves and the holiday or special occasion stress. Relax and enjoy your family and friends.

Easy Turkey Dinner

Oranged-Stuffed Roast Turkey 154
Pam's Creamy Cranberry Mold 99
Green Beans Amandine 124
Carrot Cake 201
Cream Cheese Frosting For Carrot Cake 201

Easy Chicken Dinner

Apricot-Chicken 145
Skinny Mashed Potatoes 110
Romaine Lettuce-Artichoke Salad 90
Buttermilk Biscuits 74
Cran-Grapefruit Fizz 59
Cherry Chocolate Cake 206

Ladies Summer Get-Together

Leave the kids at the club pool or with friends and kick back for an afternoon with the girls. Here's a light, fun lunch that's easy to put together, no stressful serving requirements, just casual fun and lots of time to talk

Menu #1

Menu #2

Romantic Dinners
for
Special Occasions

Whether you're having a romantic dinner for two or family and friends for a special occasion, you want to serve the best and have everyone remember the food and have a special memory. These are great choices for special memories.

Menu #1

Caviar Spread 44
Spinach, Apple & Walnut Salad 88
Sour Cream Rolls 71
Rosemary-Roasted Potatoes......................... 109
Snow Peas.. 127
Honey-Orange Glazed Chicken 137
or

Chicken Dijon 138
Key Lime Pie 232

Menu #2

Shrimp & Spinach Salad 89
Caviar Potatoes 111
Basil Green Beans 124
Herbed Pork Tenderloin 183
or

Broiled T-Bone Steaks 166
Chocolate-Covered Strawberries 210

How to Throw a Party In 10 Minutes!

If you work fast, you can make the first 3 appetizers and lime punch in 10 minutes. You might want to make the cookies the night before. This menu works for a birthday party, for a friend or relative, for a baby shower or even a Halloween party.

Beef-Cheese Ball 25
Red Cabbage Basket Dip 21
Shrimp Surprise 31
Lime Punch 56
Miracle Peanut Butter Cookies 216

If you want to invite a crowd, you may want to bake a ham, slice it and serve it on mini-egg roll buns, biscuits or party rye bread.

The night before you might want to bake Mrs. Truman's Coconut Balls, Chocolate Peanut Butter Tarts, and the Chocolate Chip Bars. You may even want to double or triple recipes.

Honey Ham 184
Mrs. Truman's Coconut Balls 229
Chocolate Chip Bars 220
Chocolate Peanut Butter Tarts 223

Appetizers
& Beverages

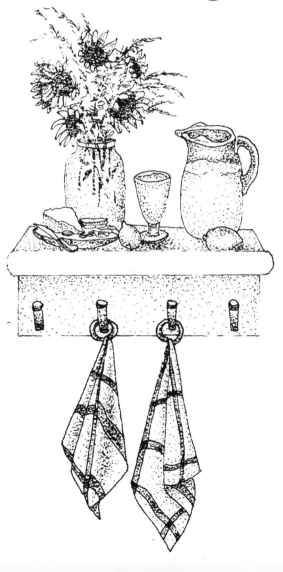

Men's Favorite Pepperoni Dip

1 (8 ounce) package pepperoni
1 pint sour cream
¼ teaspoon seasoned salt

Finely chop pepperoni, then mix with sour cream and seasoned salt. Cover and refrigerate for 2 days to allow flavors to mellow and the pepperoni to soften. Serve in a hollowed out loaf of bread, surrounded by chunks of the bread for dipping.

Hamburger Cheese Dip

1 (32 ounce) box Velveeta cheese, cubed
1 (10 ounce) can tomatoes and green chilies, drained
1 pound hamburger, browned, drained

Melt cheese with the tomatoes and green chilies. Stir in meat. Serve hot with large corn chips.

Hot Chili Dip

1 (15 ounce) can chili (no beans)
1 (4 ounce) can chopped green chilies, drained
1 (8 ounce) package grated cheddar cheese

Combine all ingredients and mix well. Microwave on high until bubbly or bake at 350° for 30 minutes. Serve with tortilla chips.

18

Tamale Dip

1 (15 ounce) can tamales
2 (15 ounce) cans chili
1 (8 ounce) package shredded cheddar cheese

Mash tamales with a fork and mix with chili. Place in a 9-inch glass pie plate. Sprinkle cheddar cheese over tamale-chili mixture. Heat in a 350° oven for about 25 minutes or until bubbly. Serve with corn chips.

Taco Dip

1 (8 ounce) package cream cheese, softened
1 (8 ounce) carton sour cream
1 (1¼ ounce) package taco seasoning mix

Beat cream cheese until creamy. Combine all ingredients, mixing well. Cover and refrigerate. Serve with corn chips.

Optional: Add 4 chopped, green onions.

Mexico City Dip

2 cups sour cream
1½ cups thick and chunky salsa
4 green onions, chopped

Combine the sour cream, salsa and green onions; mix well. Chill. Serve with corn chips.

Crock Pot Mexican Dip

1 pound pork sausage
2 (16 ounce) boxes Velveeta cheese, cubed
1 (10 ounce) can tomatoes and green chilies, drained

Brown sausage in a skillet and crumble; drain well. Place all ingredients in crock pot and heat thoroughly. Serve hot with tortilla chips.

Vegetable Dip

1 cup cottage cheese, drained
1 cup mayonnaise
1 package ranch-style salad dressing mix

Combine all ingredients and refrigerate until ready to serve. Serve with your favorite vegetables.

Optional: Stir in 3 to 4 chopped green onions

Olive-Cheese Dip

1 (7 ounce) jar stuffed green olives, finely chopped
1 (8 ounce) package cream cheese, softened
½ cup chopped pecans

Drain olives on paper towels. Beat cream cheese until creamy. Combine olives, cream cheese and pecans. Chill. Serve with chips, crackers or bread.

Red Cabbage Basket Dip

1 (1 ounce) package dry onion soup mix
1½ cups sour cream
1 small red cabbage

Combine dry onion soup mix with sour cream. Mix the dip well and refrigerate several hours. Cut top off of a washed red cabbage. Hollow out to form a basket or cup. Make a thin, straight slice off the bottom so the cabbage will sit like a bowl. Fill with onion dip. Place in center of platter and surround it with fresh veggies such as carrot sticks, celery, olives or zucchini sticks. Serve with veggies and potato chips.

Broccoli-Mushroom Dip

1 (5 ounce) tube garlic cheese
1 (10½ ounce) can golden mushroom soup
1 (10 ounce) box frozen chopped broccoli, thawed

Melt cheese with the soup. Cook broccoli according to package directions and drain. Stir into cheese-soup mixture and heat thoroughly. Serve with raw vegetables or corn chips.

Broccoli-Cheese Dip

1 stick margarine, softened
1 (16 ounce) box Velveeta jalapeno cheese
1 (10 ounce) package frozen chopped broccoli, partially thawed

Combine margarine and cheese in saucepan on lowest heat until cheese is melted. Cook broccoli according to package directions and drain. Stir into cheese-soup mixture and heat until broccoli is hot. Serve with tortilla chips.

Artichoke Dip

1 (14 ounce) can artichoke hearts, drained, chopped
1 cup grated parmesan cheese
1 cup mayonnaise

Combine all ingredients and mix well. Pour into a greased baking dish. Bake at 350° for 20 to 30 minutes. Serve with fresh vegetables, chips or crackers.

Tuna Ball

1 (8 ounce) package cream cheese, softened
½ of (1 ounce) package dry onion soup mix
1 (6 ounce) can white albacore tuna, drained

Beat cream cheese until smooth; add soup mix and tuna. Shape into a ball. Chill 4 to 6 hours. Serve with crackers.

Crab Dip

1 (8 ounce) package cream cheese, softened
1 (6 ounce) can crabmeat, drained, flaked
1 (1 ounce) package dry onion soup mix

Beat cream cheese until creamy. Combine all ingredients and mix well. Serve with shredded wheat crackers.

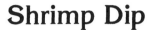

Shrimp Dip

1 (1 ounce) package dry onion soup mix
2 cups sour cream
1 cup chopped, cooked shrimp

Blend together soup mix and sour cream. Stir in chopped shrimp. Refrigerate covered for a couple hours before serving. Serve with crackers, chips, bread or veggies.

Hot Clam Dip

1 stick margarine or butter, softened
1 (8 ounce) package cream cheese, softened
1 cup clams, drained, minced

Combine and mix margarine and cream cheese in saucepan. Heat and stir until melted and smooth. Stir drained clams into mixture. Serve hot with wedges of toasted pita bread or crackers.

Optional: You may add a tiny amount of clam juice, if needed, to make mixture spreadable.

Jezebel Dip

1 (10 ounce) jar apple jelly
1 (5 ounce) jar horseradish
1 (12 ounce) jar pineapple preserves

Mix all ingredients in a saucepan until melted. Cool. Serve with ham cubes, sausage balls, etc.

Guacamole

3 avocados, peeled, seeded, mashed
1 cup thick and chunky salsa
½ cup cottage cheese, drained

Combine all ingredients, mixing well. Refrigerate. Serve as a salad with Mexican food or as a dip with tortilla chips.

Chili Con Queso

1 (1 pound) carton Velveeta cheese, cubed
1 (10 ounce) can tomatoes with green chilies, drained
2 green onions, chopped

Melt cheese in top of double boiler with the drained tomatoes. Place in serving dish. Sprinkle chopped green onions or chives over top. Serve with corn chips.

Cheesy Chicken Ball

2 (8 ounce) packages cream cheese, softened
2 (6 ounce) cans chunk white chicken,
drained, finely shredded
Garlic salt

Beat cream cheese until smooth. Combine cream cheese and chicken; blend well. Add garlic salt to taste. Shape into a ball. Serve with crackers.

Optional: As a special touch, you may want to roll in chopped pecans.

Easy Cheese Ball

2 (5 ounce) jars old English sharp cheese, softened
2 (3 ounce) packages cream cheese, softened
1 cup finely chopped nuts

Combine cheese and cream cheese in mixing bowl and beat well. Shape into a ball and chill 4 to 6 hours. Roll cheese ball in chopped nuts. Wrap in plastic wrap until time to serve. Serve with crackers, chips or breads.

Beef-Cheese Ball

1 (8 ounce) package cream cheese, softened
1 bunch green onions, finely chopped
2 jars dried beef, chopped finely

Beat cream cheese until smooth. Combine all ingredients and mix well. Shape into a ball. Refrigerate. Serve with crackers, chips or bread.

Optional: You may roll ball in ½ cup of finely chopped pecans.

Sausage Balls

2 cups biscuit mix
1 (1 pound) package hot pork sausage
1 cup shredded cheddar cheese

Combine all ingredients with a wooden spoon or your hands. Shape into balls. Place on jelly-roll pan and bake at 350° for 20 minutes. These freeze well.

Sausage-Chestnut Balls

**1 pound hot pork sausage
1 (8 ounce) can sliced water chestnuts, drained
1 cup barbecue sauce**

Shape sausage into small balls. Cut water chestnuts in half and put one chestnut half in middle of each sausage ball. Place on a greased cookie sheet and bake at 400° for 20 minutes. Drain and place in serving dish; pour heated barbecue sauce over sausage balls. Use wooden picks to serve.

Sausage-Cheese Balls

**1 (8 ounce) jar Cheez Whiz
1 pound sausage
1½ cups flour**

Mix ingredients together. Shape into small balls and bake at 350° to 375° for 15 to 20 minutes or until brown.

Optional: Try hot sausage or Mexican Cheez Whiz to give it a little heat.

Raspberry-Cheese Ball

**2 (8 ounce) packages cream cheese, softened
4 tablespoons raspberry preserves
1 cup finely chopped pecans**

Beat cream cheese until creamy. Mix cream cheese and raspberry preserves until well blended. Shape into a ball and roll in chopped pecans. Serve with crackers.

26

Stuffed Mushrooms

1 pound pork sausage
½ (1 ounce) package dry onion soup mix
1 pound large mushrooms

Combine sausage and dry onion soup mix. Break mushroom stems off. Stuff a teaspoon of sausage mixture into the cavity. Place on a baking sheet with sides. Bake at 350° for 20 minutes. Drain well before serving.

Optional: You may want to chop some of the stems and add to sausage mixture.

Bacon-Stuffed Mushrooms

1 pound fresh large mushrooms
1 (8 ounce) package cream cheese, softened
8 slices bacon, fried crisp, crumbled

Clean mushrooms and remove stems. Beat cream cheese until creamy. Mix cream cheese and crumbled, fried bacon. Stuff mushrooms with mixture. Place on a foil-lined cookie sheet and bake at 300° for 5 to 10 minutes or until hot. Broil a few seconds to brown.

Spinach-Stuffed Mushrooms

24 large mushrooms, stems removed
1 (12 ounce) package frozen spinach souffle, thawed
½ cup grated cheddar cheese

Arrange mushroom caps on a lightly greased baking sheet. Spoon a teaspoon of the spinach souffle into each mushroom cap. Top with ½ teaspoon cheese. Preheat oven to 375° and bake mushrooms for 20 minutes.

Salami Wedges

2 (8 ounce) package cream cheese, softened
4 tablespoons horseradish
36 thin salami slices

Beat cream cheese until smooth. Combine cream cheese and horseradish; mixing well. Spread on salami slices. Make 3 decker sandwiches (one slice on top of the other). Refrigerate for 1 hour. Cut into wedges or quarters and spear with wooden picks.

Wiener Kabobs

1 package wieners, cut in 1-inch pieces
1 (8 ounce) jar maraschino cherries, drained
1 (16 ounce) can pineapple chunks, drained

Alternate wieners, cherries and pineapple on 10½-inch skewers. Place on a cold broiler pan and broil for 2 minutes. Turn.

Optional: You may also brush with currant jelly. Broil for 1 minute
          longer.

Little Smokey Crescents

1 (8 ounce) can refrigerated crescent rolls
24 little smokies
1 cup barbecue sauce

Unroll crescent roll dough and spread out flat. Cut the 8 triangles lengthwise into 3 triangles each, so you'll have 24. Starting at the wide end of each dough triangle, place one smokey on dough and roll up. Repeat. Place rolls on baking sheet and bake at 400° for 10 to 15 minutes or until golden brown. Serve with barbecue sauce.

On Top Of Old Smokey

2 pounds little smokies sausages
1 pound bacon
1 (1 pound) box brown sugar

Cut smokies into 1-inch lengths and bacon slices into halves. Wrap smokies in bacon halves and secure with wooden picks. Place in a baking dish and top with brown sugar evenly spread over smokies. Bake at 350° until sugar melts, then broil until bacon browns.

Saucy Barbecued Sausages

1 (18 ounce) bottle barbecue sauce
1 (12 ounce) jar grape jelly
2 (16 ounce) packages cocktail sausages

Pour the barbecue sauce and the grape jelly into a large saucepan. Cook and stir until the jelly has melted and the mixture is smooth. Add the cooked sausage and heat on low or simmer for 20 minutes, stirring often. Serve hot. This could be served in a crock pot.

Optional: Cocktail wieners could be substituted for the sausage.

Apricot Smokies

½ cup apricot preserves
1 tablespoon prepared mustard
1 package little smokies sausages

In a saucepan, combine and heat apricot preserves and mustard. Add smokies. Heat until bubbly. Pour into serving dish. Serve with wooden picks.

Sweet N' Sour Vienna Sausages

1 (6 ounce) jar prepared mustard
1 (10 ounce) jar currant jelly
4 cans vienna sausages, drained, halved

Mix mustard and jelly in saucepan. Heat until well mixed and smooth. Add sausages and heat through. Serve in chafing dish with wooden picks.

Optional: Hot dogs or little smokies, cut in bite-size pieces, may be substituted for vienna sausages.

Salami Roll-Ups

1 (8 ounce) package cream cheese, softened
¼ pound thinly sliced salami
Green olives, chopped

Spread cream cheese evenly over salami slices. Sprinkle olives over cream cheese and press in. Roll-up and secure with wooden picks.

Shrimp Surprise

1 (8 ounce) package cream cheese
½ cup shrimp cocktail sauce
2 (4 ounce) cans tiny shrimp, cooked, drained, chilled

Place cream cheese in center of a serving plate. Pour cocktail sauce over cheese. Sprinkle chilled shrimp over sauce. Serve with crackers, surrounding shrimp dip.

Bacon-Wrapped Shrimp

1 pound large shrimp, deveined
½ teaspoon garlic powder
1 pound bacon, sliced, halved

Wash shrimp and pat dry with paper towels. Sprinkle garlic powder over shrimp, then wrap each shrimp with bacon half. Arrange on a foil-lined broiler pan and broil for 8 minutes or until bacon is crisp. Turn shrimp occasionally to brown on both sides.

Oysters In Jackets

Bacon slices, cut in halves
Large drained oysters
Small thin rounds of bread or party rye bread, toasted

Wrap each bacon half around oysters. Secure with wooden picks if needed. Place in greased pan. Bake at 400° until bacon is crispy. Remove wooden picks and serve on toast rounds.

Fish Nibbles

16 frozen, fried fish sticks, cut into thirds
½ cup grated parmesan cheese
2 tablespoons margarine

Roll fried fish pieces in parmesan cheese. Melt margarine in a jelly-roll pan. Spread evenly over bottom of pan. Arrange fish in pan and bake at 450° for 8 to 10 minutes. Turn fish and bake for 8 to 10 minutes longer or until crisp and browned. Drain on paper towels. Serve with shrimp cocktail sauce, if desired.

Fried Oat Cereal

½ cup margarine
3 cups doughnut-shaped oat cereal
Garlic salt to taste

Melt margarine in a skillet. Add cereal and stir until well coated. Cover and cook on low until crisp, about 12 to 15 minutes, stirring often. Add garlic salt. Pour on foil and separate to cool. Store in airtight cookie tin container. Serve as a snack.

Note: You may use as croutons on salads.

Cheese Chex

5 tablespoons butter
6 cups corn chex
⅓ cup fresh grated parmesan cheese

Melt butter in a large saucepan. Add corn chex and stir well. Add cheese and mix over low heat until melted. Pour out on foil and separate to cool.

Cheese Fondue

1 (1 pound) box Mexican Velveeta cheese, cubed
1 (10½ ounce) can cheese soup
1 (6 to 8 inch) round loaf bread

In a saucepan, melt cheese with cheese soup, stirring constantly to prevent scorching. Cut the center from the bread in cubes, remove and form a bowl. Place bread bowl on a platter. Pour cheese fondue into bread bowl. Surround bread bowl with bread cubes. Use cubes to dip into fondue. You can eat the bowl also.

Cheese Straws

1 (5 ounce) package pie crust mix
½ cup shredded cheddar cheese
½ teaspoon red pepper

Prepare pie crust dough according to package directions. Roll out dough on a floured board into a rectangular shape. Sprinkle cheese over dough, then sprinkle red pepper over cheese. Fold dough over once to cover cheese, then roll out again to a rectangle, ¼-inch thick. Cut dough into 3 x ½-inch strips and place them on a lightly greased cookie sheet. Bake at 350° for 10 to 15 minutes.

Cheese Squares

1 (2 pound) box Velveeta cheese
1 cup finely chopped nuts
3-5 teaspoons Tabasco

Melt cheese in top of double boiler over hot water. Stir in nuts and hot sauce; mixing well. Pour into a greased 9 x 13-inch pan. Chill until firm. Cut into squares. Serve with crackers.

Cheese Sticks

1 (5 ounce) glass Old English Cheese
1 stick margarine
1 loaf French bread, unsliced

Combine cheese and margarine; beat until smooth and soft enough to spread. Slice bread 1-inch thick. Remove crusts. Cut each into 3 sticks. Spread 3 sides and ends with cheese mixture. Bake at 350° for 10 minutes.

Hint: Cube the bread crusts that were removed and toss them with margarine and garlic salt. Bake until brown to use as croutons.

Cheese Wedges

1 (10 ounce) package refrigerated biscuits
¼ cup margarine, melted
¾ cup finely shredded cheddar cheese

Cut each biscuit into 4 wedges. Roll in the melted margarine and then the cheese. Bake at 400° for 10 minutes.

Yield: 40 wedges.

Baked Lacy Cheese

2 (8 ounce) wedges monterey jack cheese
Non-stick cooking spray
Crackers

Thinly slice or cube cheese. Spray a jelly-roll pan with non-stick cooking spray. Place small cubes of cheese on pan 2-inches apart. Bake at 400° for 2 to 3 minutes until melted and lacy. Chill. Serve with crackers or with seedless grapes.

Wrapped Gouda Cheese

1 (8 ounce) package crescent roll dough
1 (7 ounce) round gouda cheese, peeled
Melted margarine

Shape dough into a square. Wrap the dough around the peeled cheese round. Pinch edges together at the top. Brush with melted margarine. Bake at 375° for about 12 minutes. Let set for 30 minutes before slicing. Slice in thin wedges.

Baked Brie

1 round baby brie
Apricot preserves
Slivered almonds, toasted

Coat brie with preserves and bake at 350° for 20 minutes. Sprinkle with almonds. Serve with sliced apples and pears or pumpernickel bread.

Mary Sutton's Salami-Olive Wraps

8 salami slices
2 (3 ounce) packages cream cheese, softened
1 (5¾ ounce) jar stuffed green olives

Spread each salami slice with softened cream cheese. Cut salami into 4 strips. Place one olive in center of salami strip. Roll up and hold with wooden pick.

Bacon Wraps

8 bacon slices
12 tater tots
12 smoked cocktail sausages

Cut 4 bacon slices into thirds. Wrap the bacon slices around the tater tots. Arrange in a circle on paper towel-lined platter. Cover with paper towel and microwave on high for 3 minutes. Rotate plate ¼ turn and microwave until bacon is crisp, for about 2 to 4 minutes. Repeat with the 12 smoked, cocktail sausages and microwave the same way.

Baked Canadian Bacon Sandwiches

1 (5 pound) stick Canadian bacon
Dijon mustard
Party rye bread or thin sliced white bread

Wrap Canadian bacon loosely in foil. Bake in a shallow pan at 325° for 1½ hours. Slice bacon very thin. Spread mustard on bread, add bacon and serve.

Glazed Ham Cubes

⅓ cup chunky peanut butter
1 large slice cooked ham
⅓ cup packed brown sugar

Spread peanut butter over ham slice. Sprinkle brown sugar over top. Place ham under broiler for 2 to 3 minutes or until peanut butter and sugar form a brown crust. Place ham on a cutting board and cut into 1-inch squares. Serve hot on wooden picks.

Cocktail Ham

1 cup hickory-flavored barbecue sauce
4 tablespoons light brown sugar
1 pound deli ham, cut in squares

Pour barbecue sauce and sugar into a saucepan, mixing well. Heat and dissolve sugar in barbecue sauce. Add ham and heat thoroughly. Let cool. Reheat. (This improves the flavor.) Place in a chafing dish. Serve with cocktail-size hamburger buns.

Chili Snacks

1 (15 ounce) can chili without beans
1 cup shredded cheddar cheese
Party rye bread slices

Combine chili and cheese in a saucepan; heat until hot and cheese is melted. Spread on party rye bread. If desired, place bread on cookie sheet and bake at 350° for 15 to 20 minutes.

Sticky Chicky

30 chicken wings
½ cup honey
½ cup soy sauce

Wash wings and cut into sections. Discard tips. Spray 9 x 13-inch pan, pour in honey and soy sauce and mix in the pan. Arrange wings over mixture and refrigerate for 2 hours. Turn after 1 hour, so both sides will be "sticky". Bake in the same pan at 375° for 45 minutes, turning occasionally.

Chicken Nuggets

4 boneless, skinless chicken breasts
1 (5 ounce) can evaporated skim milk
Crushed potato chips

Bake chicken at 350° for about 1 hour or until tender. Cool. Cut into nugget-size pieces. Dip in milk, then roll in crushed potato chips and bake at 350° until golden brown.

Sausage-Cheese Snacks

40 slices party rye bread
1 pound hot spicy sausage
1 pound block cheddar cheese

Freeze bread. Spread raw sausage on top of bread slices. Top with slice of cheese. Lay on greased cookie sheet with edges or on a jelly-roll pan. Bake at 350° for 20 minutes.

Ham and Cheese Pick-Ups

1 (8 ounce) package cream cheese, softened
1 (1 ounce) package dry onion soup mix
2 (3 ounce) packages thin sliced ham

Beat cream cheese until creamy; stir in onion soup mix.
(You may need to add a little mayonnaise or milk to make
cream cheese easier to spread.) Lay out slices of ham and
carefully spread a thin layer of cream cheese mixture over
each slice of ham. Roll ham slices into a log. Refrigerate an
hour or two. When ready to serve, slice into ¾-inch slices.
Place wooden pick in each slice for easy pick-up.

Ann's Bacon-Wrapped Chestnuts

1 (8 ounce) can whole water chestnuts, drained
¼ cup soy sauce
½ pound bacon, halved

Marinate water chestnuts for 1 hour or more in soy sauce.
Wrap ½ bacon slice around chestnut and fasten with a
wooden pick. Bake at 375° for 20 to 25 minutes.

Speedy Jalapeno Appetizers

1 (8 ounce) package cream cheese, softened
2 tubes Ritz crackers
1 (10 ounce) jar green jalapeno jelly

Spread softened cream cheese on crackers. Spoon a small
amount of jalapeno jelly in the middle of each cracker. Serve
immediately.

Eggplant Porcupine

1 large eggplant
Cheddar cheese, cubed
Olives

Cut slice from an eggplant bottom so it will stand upright. Place in center of a dish. Thread cheese cube, olive and second cheese cube on wooden picks. Insert in eggplant. Completely cover until the eggplant looks like a porcupine full of quills.

Olive Wraps

1 can buttermilk biscuits
1 (5¾ ounce) jar stuffed green olives
Parmesan cheese

Cut each biscuit into quarters. Wrap dough around one olive. Roll in grated parmesan cheese. Place on greased cookie sheet and bake at 350° for 6 to 8 minutes.

Baked Cheese Souffle Sandwiches

1 pound margarine, softened
3 (5 ounce) jars Old English cheese spread, softened
1½ loaves bread

Blend margarine and cheese for 5 minutes with an electric mixer. Remove bread crusts. Spread cheese on bread to make sandwiches. Stack 2 slices of bread together and cut each stack into 4 sections. Frost each stack with cheese mixture and bake at 350° for 15 minutes. These can be frozen.

Pecan Bites

1 (8 ounce) package cream cheese, softened
¼ pound blue cheese
80 pecan halves

Several hours before serving, mix cream cheese and blue cheese in mixer; beat until creamy. Cover and refrigerate. Shape into 40 balls and press a pecan on both sides of ball. Refrigerate until ready to serve.

Chinese Chicken Wings

3 pounds chicken wings
1 (10 ounce) bottle soy sauce
½ cup sugar

Clean wings, snip tips and discard. Mix soy sauce and sugar in a 9 x 13 x 2-inch glass dish or pan. Add chicken wings, turn to coat. Marinate wings for 24 hours in the refrigerator. Turn often. Remove from refrigerator after 24 hours. Let set on counter for 15 minutes. Pour off most of sauce. Cover dish tightly with foil. Bake at 250° for 2 hours. Remove foil during last 15 minutes of baking time to brown wings.

Ham-Stuffed Tomatoes

1 pint cherry tomatoes
2 (2¼ ounce) cans deviled ham
2 tablespoon horseradish

About 3 hours before serving, slice tops from tomatoes. Scoop out pulp and mix with ham and horseradish. Fill tomatoes. Refrigerate about 3 hours.

Stuffed Cherry Tomatoes

1 (8 ounce) package cream cheese, softened
½ onion, very finely chopped
12 cherry tomatoes

Beat cream cheese until creamy. Combine cream cheese
and onion; mixing well. Cut tomatoes in half. Drain on
paper towels. Scoop out pulp and mix into cream cheese.
Stuff tomatoes with cream cheese mixture. Cover and chill.

Taco Meatballs

1 (2 pound) package hamburger or ground round
2 eggs, beaten
1 (1¼ ounce) package taco seasoning mix

Combine all ingredients and mix and shape into small
meatballs. Place in a foil-lined pan and bake at 375° for
about 15 minutes or until brown. Drain. Serve on wooden
picks.

Ham Pinwheels

9 thin slices cooked ham
1 (5 ounce) jar olive-pimento spread
9 pickle sticks

Spread thin slices of cooked ham with olive-pimento spread.
Lay a pickle stick on the ham, then roll up. Slice or serve as
pinwheels. Secure with wooden picks.

Tuna Fish Spread

1 (6 ounce) can tuna fish, drained, flaked
6 tablespoons sour cream
½ (1 ounce) package dry onion soup mix

Combine all ingredients, mixing well. Spread on bread. Trim crusts. Serve as open face sandwiches, finger sandwiches or ribbon sandwiches.

Shrimp Spread

1 (6 ounce) can shrimp, drained, mashed
1 (3 ounce) package cream cheese, softened
Shrimp cocktail sauce

Combine mashed shrimp and mashed cream cheese. Mix until well blended. Stir in enough shrimp cocktail sauce for spreading consistency. Spread on crackers.

Crabmeat Spread

1 (8 ounce) package cream cheese, softened
1 (6 ounce) can crabmeat, well drained, flaked
½ (8 ounce) bottle seafood cocktail sauce

Spread softened, cream cheese on a 10-inch serving plate. Spread drained crabmeat over the cheese, then cover with cocktail sauce. Cover with plastic wrap and refrigerate for 4 hours. Serve with crackers.

Caviar Spread

1 (8 ounce) package cream cheese
½ red onion, finely chopped
1 (2 ounce) jar black caviar

Place the cream cheese in the center of a plate. Sprinkle the chopped red onion over cheese, then heap caviar on top. Serve with melba toast rounds.

Curried Almonds

1 tablespoon margarine
8 ounces raw almonds
1 teaspoon curry powder

In a skillet, melt margarine and saute almonds until they are slightly colored. Season with curry powder to taste. Mix well. Serve warm.

Microwave-Buttered Walnuts

1 pound walnut halves
1 teaspoon seasoned salt
¼ cup margarine or butter

Place walnuts in a 1½-quart microwave-safe dish. Add salt and dot with margarine or butter. Microwave on high power for 1 to 2 minutes. Stir until butter coats nuts evenly.

Spicy Peanuts

2 teaspoons vegetable oil
1½ teaspoons ground red pepper
2 cups dry roasted peanuts

Heat oil in a 10-inch skillet over medium heat. Stir in red pepper and peanuts. Mix and cook 2 minutes, stirring constantly until evenly coated and hot.

Lucy Hetzel's Fresh Fruit Dip

1 (8 ounce) package cream cheese, softened
1 (7 ounce) jar marshmallow creme
¼ teaspoon ginger

Beat cream cheese until smooth. Combine all ingredients and mix well. Serve with your favorite fresh fruits, such as strawberries, banana slices or apple slices, surrounding dip.

Orange-Fruit Dip

1 (8 ounce) package cream cheese, softened
½ cup chopped pecans
1½ tablespoons dry orange drink mix

Beat cream cheese until creamy. Combine all ingredients and mix well; chill. Serve in small bowl in the middle of a platter surrounded by sliced apples.

Hint: Slice off top of an orange. Scoop the pulp from the fruit. Fill the fruit cup with the dip.

Strawberries and Dip

1 (8 ounce) carton sour cream
2 tablespoons brown sugar
Fresh strawberries, chilled

Combine sour cream and brown sugar; mix well. Serve in a
bowl in the middle of a platter surrounded by fresh
strawberries.

Strawberry-Fruit Dip

1 (8 ounce) package cream cheese, softened
1 (8 ounce) jar strawberry preserves
1 (8 ounce) carton whipped topping, thawed

In mixer bowl, combine cream cheese and preserves; whip
until smooth. Fold in whipped topping and blend well. Serve
as a dip with apples and strawberries.

Strawberry Spritzer Punch

3 (10 ounce) packages frozen strawberries, thawed, divided
2 (24 ounce) bottles white grape juice, chilled
1 (28 ounce) bottle club soda or carbonated water, chilled

Place 2 packages of thawed strawberries with juice in a
blender. Cover and blend until smooth. In a punch bowl,
combine berries, grape juice and remaining package of
strawberries; mix well. When ready to serve, stir in
carbonated water.

Strawberry Punch

2 (10 ounce) boxes frozen strawberries
1 (12 ounce) can frozen pink lemonade concentrate,
diluted, chilled
1 (2 liter) bottle 7-Up or ginger ale, chilled

Thaw berries until slushy; mix in blender. Pour lemonade
into punch bowl and stir in berries. Add 7-Up or ginger ale
and stir until well blended. If this punch is too tart, you can
add sugar.

Strawberry Cooler

1 (6 ounce) can frozen limeade concentrate, diluted
1 (10 ounce) package frozen strawberries, thawed
1 (2 liter) bottle strawberry-carbonated beverage, chilled

Prepare limeade by diluting it according to directions on the
can. Chill. Blend berries in a blender until smooth.
Combine limeade and berries in a punch bowl. When ready
to serve, stir in strawberry-carbonated beverage.

Orange-Strawberry Drink

2 cups orange juice, chilled
1½ cups apricot nectar, chilled
1 cup frozen sweetened strawberries, thawed

Combine all ingredients in blender and mix well.

Anna Marie's Low-Cal Punch

1 (2 liter) diet 7-Up, chilled
1 (12 ounce) can frozen lemonade, diluted
1 (46 ounce) can unsweetened pineapple juice, chilled

Combine all ingredients in punch bowl and mix well. You can also add an ice ring to the punch bowl.

Yield: about 22 cups.

Party Fruit Punch

2 quarts cranberry juice, chilled
1 (46 ounce) can fruit punch, chilled
1 (46 ounce) can pineapple juice, chilled

Pour 1-quart cranberry juice into ice trays and freeze as ice cubes. In punch bowl, combine the fruit punch, pineapple juice and 1-quart cranberry juice; mixing well. When ready to serve, add cranberry ice cubes.

Cranberry Punch

2 quarts cranberry juice, chilled
2 quarts ginger ale or 7-Up, chilled
1 (12 ounce) can frozen lemonade concentrate

Combine, mix and pour all ingredients into punch bowl. Add 2 cans ice water.

Mary's D.A.R. Punch

2 quarts orange juice, chilled
2 quarts lemonade, chilled
1 (2 liter) bottle 7-Up, chilled

Combine and mix in a punch bowl.

Christmas Punch

1 (46 ounce) can pineapple juice, chilled
1 (1 liter) bottle ginger ale, chilled
1 (2 liter) bottle strawberry-carbonated beverage, chilled

Combine all ingredients in punch bowl. Use extra ginger ale or 7-Up, if desired. Makes about 20 servings.

Holiday Punch

1 package cherry fruit-flavored drink mix
2 quarts ginger ale, chilled
1 (46 ounce) can pineapple juice, chilled

Combine all ingredients and mix well. Add more ginger ale if needed. Serve in punch bowl.

Emerald Punch

2 packages lime fruit-flavored drink mix
1 (46 ounce) can pineapple juice, chilled
1 (2 liter) bottle ginger ale, chilled

Prepare drink mix according to package directions. Chill several hours. Pour into punch bowl. Stir in pineapple juice. When ready to serve, add ginger ale.

Hint: Make an ice ring of additional ginger ale and add to punch bowl. If you don't have a round jello mold, pour ginger ale into any nicely shaped container and freeze.

Orange Grapefruit Cooler

1 (46 ounce) can grapefruit juice, chilled
1 (46 ounce) can orange juice, chilled
1 (2 liter) bottle ginger ale, chilled

Combine and mix juices in punch bowl. Add ginger ale when ready to serve.

Pineapple Slush Punch

1 (46 ounce) can pineapple juice, chilled
1 (46 ounce) can apple juice, chilled
2 (28 ounce) bottles 7-Up, chilled

Freeze pineapple juice and apple juice in their cans. Set out juices about 30 minutes to 1 hour before serving. When ready to serve, combine all ingredients in a punch bowl.

Five Alive Punch

2 (12 ounce) cans frozen Five Alive juice concentrate
1 (12 ounce) can frozen pink lemonade concentrate
1 (2 liter) bottle ginger ale, chilled

Dilute juices as directed on the cans, then mix together in a punch bowl. When ready to serve, add in ginger ale.

Pina Colada Punch

1 (2 quart) can pineapple-coconut juice, chilled
2 quarts 7-Up, chilled
1 (20 ounce) can pineapple rings, drained, reserve juice

Combine pineapple-coconut juice, 7-Up and juice from pineapple rings in a punch bowl. Float pineapple rings in punch bowl.

Betty's Hawaiian Punch

1 (46 ounce) can Hawaiian Punch, chilled
1 (2 liter) bottle ginger ale or 7-Up, chilled
1 (12 ounce) can frozen lemonade concentrate

Combine the ingredients in a punch bowl. Mix in 2 cups cold water. Serve immediately. Serves 22 cups of punch.

Pink Grapefruit Punch

1 (46 ounce) can pink grapefruit juice, chilled
1 (46 ounce) can pineapple juice, chilled
1 (1 liter) bottle 7-Up, chilled

Mix juices and 7-Up together in a punch bowl. Serve immediately.

Onita Copeland's Grape Punch

1 cup red seedless grapes in a frozen ice ring of ginger ale
1 gallon white grape juice, chilled
½ gallon ginger ale, chilled

When ready to serve, mix juice and ginger ale in punch bowl. Add ice ring.

Mocha Punch

1 quart coffee, chilled
1 quart chocolate milk
1 quart vanilla or chocolate ice cream

Mix the coffee and milk together until well blended. Just before serving, stir in the ice cream and mix until creamy.

Spritely Punch

1 gallon Sprite, chilled
½ gallon pineapple juice, chilled
1 gallon orange sherbet

Combine Sprite and juice in punch bowl. Spoon in sherbet and mix well.

English Tea Punch

1 (12 ounce) can frozen orange juice, thawed
½ gallon prepared lemon tea, chilled
1 (46 ounce) can pineapple juice, chilled

Dilute orange juice according to directions on the can. Combine all ingredients in a punch bowl and stir.

Dorothy Townsend's Strawberry Punch

½ gallon strawberry ice cream, softened
2 (2 liter) bottles ginger ale or 7-Up, chilled
1 (10 ounce) package frozen strawberries, thawed

Combine all ingredients in a punch bowl and stir well. Serve immediately. Makes about 26 punch cups.

Barbara's Pineapple Punch

4 quarts ginger ale, chilled
2 quarts pineapple sherbet
1 (15 ounce) can pineapple tidbits, chilled

Combine ginger ale, pineapple sherbet and pineapple tidbits. Mix. Serve in punch bowl. Makes about 28 (4 ounce) cups.

Apricot Orange Punch

1 (46 ounce) can apricot juice, chilled
1 (2 liter) bottle ginger ale, chilled
½ gallon orange sherbet

When ready to serve, combine juice and ginger ale in a punch bowl. Stir in scoops of orange sherbet. Serve in 4-ounce punch cups. Makes about 35 cups.

Cranberry Cream Punch

1 cup cranberry juice cocktail, chilled
1 large scoop vanilla ice cream
1 (8 ounce) vanilla yogurt

Combine all ingredients. Serve in sherbet glasses or punch cups.

Cranberry-Grape Frost

1 (48 ounce) bottle cranberry juice, chilled
1 (46 ounce) can grape juice, chilled
½ gallon raspberry sherbet

Combine cranberry and grape juices in a punch bowl. Add scoops of raspberry sherbet and mix well.

Optional: Add 1 (2 liter) bottle chilled ginger ale or 7-Up if you want to add something extra.

Lemonade

2 cups lemon juice (about 8 lemons)
6 cups water
1 cup sugar

Combine all ingredients in a 2-quart pitcher and mix until sugar is dissolved. Serve over ice.

Yield: 8 servings.

Limeade

4-6 large limes, squeezed
1 cup sugar
2 quarts water

Rinse limes. Roll on cutting board or on the counter to soften, then cut in half. Squeeze juice. Combine juice, sugar and water in a pitcher and stir until sugar is dissolved.

Yield: 6 to 8 servings.

Lime Punch

2 (2 liter) bottles 7-Up, chilled
1 (2 liter) bottle ginger ale, chilled
½ gallon lime sherbet

Combine 7-Up and ginger ale. When ready to serve, add lime sherbet. Stir until well mixed. Serve in punch cups.

Frosty Grape Punch

1 (2 quart) bottle grape juice, chilled
½ gallon raspberry sherbet
2 (2 liter) bottles ginger ale, chilled

Combine and mix grape juice and sherbet in a punch bowl. Add ginger ale when ready to serve.

Purple Passion Punch

3 quarts grape juice, chilled
1 quart cranberry juice, chilled
1 quart raspberry sherbet

Combine the two juices in a punch bowl and mix well. Stir in sherbet. Serve immediately.

Frosty Orange-Pineapple Punch

2 (46 ounce) cans pineapple juice, chilled
½ gallon orange sherbet
1 (2 liter) bottle ginger ale, chilled

Pour juice in punch bowl and stir in sherbet. Add ginger ale and serve immediately.

Peach Nectar Punch

1 (46 ounce) can apricot nectar, chilled
1 (2 liter) bottle peach soda, chilled
½ gallon peach ice cream

When ready to serve, combine apricot nectar and peach soda in a punch bowl. Stir in peach ice cream.

This was served at a wedding reception that I attended and I thought it was so delicious I asked for the recipe.

Agua de Sandia

4 cups cubed watermelon
½ gallon water, chilled
1 cup sugar

Place watermelon in blender. Blend at high speed until smooth. Pour in a 2-quart container. Add enough water to make 2 quarts. Add sugar and stir until dissolved.

Optional: You may substitute 4 cups fresh pineapple or the juice of 4 oranges or 4 cups frozen strawberries for the watermelon.

Hot Apple Cider

2 quarts apple cider
½ cup cinnamon red hot candies
1 apple, sliced

Pour apple cider into a large pan. Stir in red hot candies.
Simmer until candy has dissolved. Serve hot in mugs.
Garnish with ½ apple slice.

Winter Punch

1 (46 ounce) can cocktail vegetable juice, chilled
1 tablespoon lemon juice
½ teaspoon dried dill weed

Combine, mix and serve chilled in glasses.

Hint: Place a long celery stick in each glass for stirring.
Optional: Several drops of Tabasco may also be added.

Shirley Temple

4 tablespoons grenadine syrup
4 cups ginger ale, chilled
4 maraschino cherries

Put 1 tablespoon grenadine syrup in each glass. Add ginger
ale and stir. Garnish with a maraschino cherry.

Mock Pink Champagne

2 quarts cranberry juice, chilled
1 quart ginger ale, chilled
1 quart 7-Up, chilled

When ready to serve, combine cranberry juice, ginger ale and 7-Up in a punch bowl. (Don't prepare punch ahead of time.) Will serve 30 (4 ounce) punch cups.

Cran-Grapefruit Fizz

2 cups cranberry juice, chilled
2 cups club soda, chilled
1 cup pink grapefruit juice, chilled

Combine all ingredients in pitcher and mix. Serve chilled.

Sun Tea

8 (regular size) tea bags
1 gallon cold water
10 lemon slices or mint springs

Put tea bags in a gallon jar and fill with cold water. Set jar in sunshine for 3 to 4 hours. Serve over ice with lemon slice or sprig of mint.

Pineapple Tea

1 (46 ounce) can pineapple juice
2 packages sweetened, lemon-lime flavored drink mix
1 tablespoon instant tea

Place all ingredients in a gallon jar. Fill with water. Stir and allow tea to sit overnight in refrigerator. Add more tea to taste if necessary.

Refrigerator Iced Tea

8 (regular size) tea bags
2 quarts cold water
8 lemon slices

Rather than boiling water on hot, humid days, just add 8 tea bags to 2 quarts cold water. Place in refrigerator for 3 to 4 hours. Remove tea bags when ready to serve. Serve over ice with lemon slices.

Cider Tea

3 cups boiling water
2 family-size orange pekoe tea bags
3 cups apple cider

Pour boiling water over tea bags. Cover and steep for 8 minutes. Discard tea bags. Stir in cider and mix well.

Cranberry Sherbet Punch

½ gallon cranberry juice, chilled
1 quart ginger ale, chilled
½ gallon pineapple sherbet

Combine juice and ginger ale in a punch bowl. Stir in sherbet.

Carolyn Warren's Strawberry Milk Shake

½ cup fresh strawberries, sliced
½ cup skim milk
3 packets granulated sugar substitute

Combine berries, milk and sugar substitute in a blender. Blend until smooth.

Optional: To make a thicker shake, add 3 ice cubes to the blender. Also, you can substitute frozen, unsweetened berries for the fresh ones.

Fuzzy Navel Milk Shake

1 cup fresh peaches, peeled, pitted, chopped
1 cup orange juice, chilled
4 scoops vanilla ice cream

Combine all ingredients in a blender and mix well. Pour into tall glasses.

Chocolate Eggnog

1 (1 to 2 quart) cans eggnog, chilled
¼ cup chocolate sauce
Nutmeg

Combine eggnog and chocolate sauce; serve cold. Sprinkle with nutmeg. Add more chocolate sauce if desired.

Chocolate Milk Shake

1 cup milk
⅓ cup chocolate-flavored syrup
2 to 3 scoops vanilla ice cream

Place milk and syrup in blender. Cover and blend on high speed 5 seconds. Add ice cream. Cover and blend on low speed for 5 to 10 seconds. Pour into 2 glasses.

Rosebillie's Cocoa Mix

3 cups dry powdered milk
1 cup sugar
⅓ cup cocoa

Mix all ingredients together. Use 6 level tablespoons to each cup of hot water to make a cup of hot chocolate.

Optional: You may top each cup with a marshmallow.

Party
Sandwiches
& Breads

Olive-Egg Salad Spread
for Sandwiches

6 hard-boiled eggs
12 stuffed green olives, finely chopped
Mayonnaise

Rinse hard-boiled eggs in cool water. Peel off shells and chop eggs. Combine eggs, olives and enough mayonnaise to moisten. Refrigerate until ready to use. Spread on wheat bread and cut in half for sandwiches.

Pinwheel Spread for Sandwiches

1 (3 ounce) package cream cheese, softened
½ cup crushed pineapple, well drained
¼ cup finely chopped pecans

Beat cheese until light and fluffy. Stir in well-drained pineapple and pecans, mixing well.

For sandwiches: Trim crust off several slices of white bread. Roll each slice with a rolling pin to flatten. Spread with a little softened margarine, then spread pineapple filling on each slice. Roll up tightly and place each roll tightly together in a pan; wrap in plastic wrap. Refrigerate for several hours or overnight. When ready to serve, cut rolls into ¾-inch slices, then place on serving trays.

Watercress Sandwiches

20 slices thin bread
Butter or cream cheese, softened
1 bunch watercress, washed, finely chopped

Remove crusts from bread. Spread either butter or cream cheese on bread slices. Place chopped watercress on half buttered bread, then cover with remaining bread slices. Cut each sandwich into 3 bars or 4 triangles. Arrange sandwiches on a serving tray. Garnish each with tiny sprigs of watercress.

Dorothy Townsend's
Ribbon Sandwiches

8 slices sandwich bread (4 whole wheat and 4 white)
1 (5 ounce) jar Old English cheese spread
1 stick margarine, softened

Remove crusts from bread slices. With mixer, beat together the cheese spread and margarine until smooth. Spread mixture on the 4 slices of white bread. Top with the whole wheat slices. Slice each sandwich in 3 or 4 strips. Wrap tightly with cover and refrigerate.

Cream Cheese-Walnut Spread

1 (8 ounce) package cream cheese, softened
¼ cup walnuts, chopped
½ cup stuffed green olives, sliced or chopped

Beat cream cheese until smooth. Combine with walnuts and green olives. Spread on whole wheat bread.

Cucumber Tea Sandwich Spread

1 (8 ounce) package cream cheese, softened
2 cucumbers, peeled, seeded, grated
¾ teaspoon seasoned salt

Beat cream cheese until smooth. Drain grated cucumber well with several paper towels. Combine cream cheese, grated cucumbers and seasoned salt, mixing well. Spread on slices of crust-trimmed white bread slices. Cut sandwich in triangle or bars.

Dainty Checkerboard Sandwiches

1 unsliced loaf whole wheat bread
1 unsliced loaf white bread
3 (5 ounce) jars olive and cream cheese spread

Remove crusts from 2 unsliced loaves of bread. From each loaf, cut 6 lengthwise slices ½-inch thick. Spread cheese spread on bread to put 4 long slices of bread together, alternating 2 whole wheat and 2 white to make a checkerboard. Slice crosswise. Wrap in foil and refrigerate.

Yield: Two ribbon loaves make three checkerboards.

Black Olive Spread

1 (3 ounce) package cream cheese, softened
1 (2.25 ounce) can chopped black olives, drained
1 (8 ounce) package shredded cheddar cheese

Beat cream cheese until smooth. Combine olives and the 2 cheeses. Spread on slices of party rye or pumpernickel bread. Serve cold or broil and serve hot.

Optional: You may mix in 3 chopped green onions for a variation.

Cherry-Cheese Sandwich Spread

1 (8 ounce) jar maraschino cherries
1 (8 ounce) package cream cheese, softened
½ cup finely chopped pecans

Drain cherries and finely dice. Beat cream cheese until creamy. Combine cream cheese, diced cherries and pecans; mix until well blended. Trim crusts from several slices of white bread. Use filling for open-face sandwiches or make into 3-layered ribbon sandwiches.

Pimento Cheese

Makes great toasted sandwiches.

2 cups pasteurized processed cheese spread or mild cheddar cheese, grated
1 (2 ounce) jar chopped pimento, drained
Mayonnaise

Combine; mix thoroughly and chill.

Yield: 2 cups.

Party Sandwiches

1 (2¼ ounce) can deviled ham
1 tablespoon green pepper, finely chopped
1 teaspoon prepared horseradish

Combine all ingredients, mixing well. Spread ham on white bread and top with whole wheat bread. Trim off crusts. Cut sandwiches lengthwise in thirds to make bar sandwiches.

Deviled Ham Spread

1 (4½ ounce) can deviled ham
⅓ cup sour cream
⅓ cup shredded cheddar cheese

Combine all ingredients, mixing well. To make sandwiches, remove crusts from 4 slices white bread, butter lightly, then cut each slice into 4 squares. Spread ham spread on each square. Bake sandwich squares at 400° for 5 minutes or until hot and bubbly and serve as open-face sandwiches.

Chicken-Almond Sandwich

2 cups finely shredded, cooked chicken
½ cup finely chopped, toasted almonds
Mayonnaise

Combine chicken and almonds with enough mayonnaise to moisten and form a spread. For sandwiches, spread chicken filling on thinly sliced, white bread that has had the crusts removed. Cut into squares, triangles or bars.

Optional: You may also stir in ½ cup finely diced celery.

Beef Spread for Sandwiches

1 (5 ounce) jar dried beef, chopped
1 (8 ounce) carton sour cream
¾ cup shredded Swiss or cheddar cheese

Combine all ingredients, mixing well. Cover and refrigerate. Spread on white bread that has had crusts removed. Cut into finger sandwiches.

Zesty Roast Beef Party Sandwiches

1 (4 pound) beef roast
Worcestershire sauce
Mustard

Rub roast with worcestershire sauce, then with hands rub well with mustard. Bake at 350°, basting occasionally with worcestershire sauce, to desired doneness. After roast has browned, add a little water to keep it from burning, then baste with drippings. Let roast set 15 minutes before slicing. Slice very thin. Serve on tiny, sliced buns or biscuits.

Salami-On-Rye Sandwiches

24 salami slices
48 slices party rye bread
1 (8 ounce) jar dijon mustard

Place 1 slice of salami folded in half or quartered to fit on rye bread. Spread with mustard. Top with second slice of party rye for quick party sandwiches.

Yield: 24 sandwiches.

Pigs In Blankets

1 package 10 hot dogs
3 (12 ounce) cans biscuits
Dijon mustard

Cut hot dogs in thirds. Wrap in biscuit that has been spread with mustard. Bake at 425° for 8 to 10 minutes.

Yield: 30

Easy Garlic Bread

1 (1 pound) loaf French bread
½ cup butter, softened
Garlic salt or garlic powder

Cut bread diagonally into 1-inch slices. Spread with butter and sprinkle with garlic. Lay slices on a cookie sheet and bake at 425° until golden brown on both sides.

Lucy Hetzel's
Mozzarella Cheese Loaf

1 loaf unsliced French or Italian bread
Softened margarine
Sliced mozzarella cheese

Slice bread almost all the way through at ½-inch intervals. Brush the loaf generously with margarine and place mozzarella slices between the slices of bread. Place on a greased, baking sheet and bake at 450° for 10 minutes, or until cheese melts and bread is golden brown.

Hot Cheesy Bread Slices

1 (8 ounce) package shredded cheddar cheese
1 cup mayonnaise
1 loaf French bread, cut in ½-inch slices

Mix together cheese and mayonnaise. Spread on bread slices. Place bread slices on cookie sheet and bake at 350° for 8 to 10 minutes. For variety, mix 2 cheeses, cheddar and Swiss, with mayonnaise and spread on the bread.

Chili-Cheese Bread

1 loaf unsliced, French bread
1 cup shredded, cheddar cheese
1 (7 ounce) can chopped, green chilies, drained

Cut bread in half lengthwise. Spread cheddar cheese over each half. Sprinkle chopped chilies over top. Place on cookie sheet. Bake at 325° for 10 minutes.

Sour Cream Rolls

1 cups self-rising flour
½ cup melted margarine
1 cup sour cream

Combine flour, margarine and sour cream; mix. Pour into greased, miniature muffin tins and bake at 350° for 15 minutes.

Cloverleaf Rolls

2 ¼ cups biscuit mix, divided
1 (8 ounce) carton sour cream
½ cup melted margarine

Combine 2 cups biscuit mix with sour cream and melted margarine and mix well. Sprinkle the remaining ¼ cup of biscuit mix on sheet of waxed paper. Drop dough by level tablespoonfuls onto biscuit mix and roll into small balls. Place 3 balls into each of 12 greased muffin cups. Bake at 350° for 15 to 20 minutes or until golden brown.

Italian Crescent Rolls

1 (8 ounce) package refrigerated crescent rolls
¼ stick butter or margarine, melted
½ teaspoon Italian seasoning

Unroll crescent rolls and separate into 8 triangles. Brush with melted butter and sprinkle with Italian seasoning. Roll dough up, following package directions. Bake at 375° for 10 minutes or until golden brown.

Mexican Corn Bread

1 (8½ ounce) package corn bread mix
½ cup shredded cheddar cheese
1 (8 ounce) can cream-style corn

Prepare corn bread according to package directions. Stir in corn and ¼ cup shredded cheese. Pour into a greased skillet or muffin tins. Top with remaining ¼ cup cheese. Bake at 400° for 15 to 20 minutes.

Bacon Sticks

10 strips bacon
20 long, thin garlic bread sticks
Parmesan cheese

Cut bacon in half lengthwise, making 2 long thin strips from each slice. Wrap 1 strip in a spiral around each bread stick. Place in pan with a rack so the bacon drippings will go to the bottom of the pan away from the bread sticks. Bake at 350º for about 10 minutes or until bacon is almost done. Turn bread sticks over and bake until bacon is done. Remove from oven and sprinkle with cheese.

Rosebillie Horn's Zucchini Bread

1 (18.25 ounce) box spice cake mix
2 cups shredded zucchini
½ cup chopped black walnuts or pecans

Prepare cake mix according to package directions. Squeeze liquid out of zucchini, then stir zucchini and nuts into the spice cake; mix well. Pour into 2 greased and floured loaf pans. Bake at 350° for 50 to 60 minutes.

No-Peek Popovers

2 eggs
1 cup milk
1 cup flour

Combine all ingredients and mix well. Pour into 8 greased muffin cups ¾ full. Place in a cold 450° oven and bake for 30 minutes and don't peek.

Mayonnaise Rolls

2 cups self-rising flour
1 cup milk
4 tablespoons mayonnaise

Combine all ingredients; mixing well and pour into greased muffin tins. Bake at 400° for 22 minutes.

Cheese Puffs

1 (12 count) can biscuits
Cheddar cheese, cut into 12 cubes
Vegetable oil

Separate biscuits and roll out or press out flat. Place a cheese cube in the center. Shape into a ball. Drop in boiling oil. Deep fry until golden and puffy. Drain on paper towels.

Cheese Biscuits

2¼ cups baking mix
⅔ cup milk
½ cup shredded cheddar cheese

Mix all ingredients until soft dough forms. Beat for 30 seconds. If dough is too sticky, add more baking mix. Drop by rounded spoonfuls onto a greased cookie sheet and bake at 350° for 15 minutes or until lightly browned.

Buttermilk Biscuits

½ cup margarine
2 cups flour
¾ cup buttermilk

Cut ½ cup margarine into flour with a pastry blender until mixture resembles coarse meal. Stir in buttermilk and mix until dry ingredients are moistened. Turn dough out onto a floured surface and knead 3 or 4 times. Roll dough to ¾-inch thickness, then cut with a biscuit cutter. Place on a lightly greased, cookie sheet and bake at 425° for 12 to 15 minutes. Brush with additional melted margarine, if desired.

Party Biscuits

1 cup flour
1 cup whipping cream
2 tablespoons sugar

Mix all ingredients and pour into greased mini-muffin cups.
Bake 400° for 10 minutes.

Onion Biscuits

2 cups biscuit mix
¼ cup milk
1 (8 ounce) carton French onion dip

Combine all ingredients and mix until a soft dough forms.
Drop dough into mounds onto a well-greased cookie sheet.
Bake at 375° for 10 to 12 minutes or until light golden brown.
If you would like the round, cut-out biscuits, sprinkle extra
biscuit mix on a piece of waxed paper; spoon dough over
biscuit mix. Sprinkle about a tablespoon biscuit mix over
dough and knead 3 or 4 times. Use a little more biscuit mix if
dough is too sticky. Pat out to a ½-inch thickness and cut
with biscuit cutter.

Orange Biscuits

1 can refrigerated biscuits
Sugar cubes
Orange juice

Before putting biscuits in the oven to bake, put 1 sugar cube
(pressed into dough) and 1 teaspoon orange juice on each
biscuit. Bake according to biscuit directions.

Orange Butter

1 cup butter, softened
2 tablespoons grated orange rind
¼ cup orange juice

Beat butter and rind until fluffy. Gradually add orange juice and beat until well blended. Store in refrigerator. Serve with hot biscuits.

Jill Ruiz's Coffee Cake

1 loaf frozen bread, thawed
½ pint whipping cream
Sugar-cinnamon mixture

Spread dough into a greased, 9 x 13-inch pan. Let rise. Poke several times with finger. Sprinkle sugar mixture over it. Pour cream evenly over top. Bake at 350° for 20 minutes or until golden brown.

Mini-Sweet Rolls

6 teaspoons margarine, divided
6 teaspoons brown sugar, divided
1 (8 ounce) package crescent rolls

In greased, miniature, muffin pans, place ½ teaspoon margarine and ½ teaspoon brown sugar in each cup. Take 1 package crescent rolls and roll out. Take 2 squares; press together the creases. Roll up tightly. Slice each roll in 6 slices. Lay a slice in each muffin cup on top of margarine and brown sugar. Bake at 375° for 10 to 12 minutes.

Yield: 12 rolls.

Ice Cream Muffins

2 cups self-rising flour
1 pint vanilla ice cream
2½ tablespoons margarine or butter, melted

Blend together flour and ice cream until well moistened. The batter will be lumpy. Fill 10 buttered, muffin cups ¾ full. Spoon a teaspoon of melted butter over top of muffin. Bake at 350° for 20 minutes.

Yield: 5 to 10 servings.

Salads & Soups

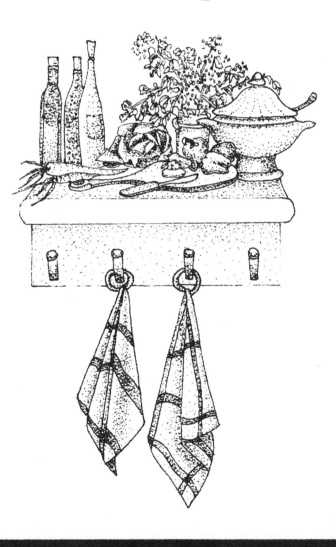

Cranberry-Apple Salad

1 (3 ounce) package cranberry gelatin
1 (16 ounce) can whole berry cranberry sauce
2 apples, peeled, chopped

Mix gelatin with 1 cup boiling water. Stir in cranberry sauce until well mixed and fold in apples. Pour into serving bowl. Cover and refrigerate until firm.

Blueberry Salad

2 (3 ounce) boxes grape gelatin
1 (20 ounce) can blueberry pie filling
1 (20 ounce) can crushed pineapple, undrained

Dissolve gelatin using 1 cup boiling water. Refrigerate until partially set, then stir in blueberries, pineapple and juice. Pour into a 9 x 13-inch glass dish and chill until firm.

Optional: You may add a sliced banana when other fruit is added.

Lime-Pineapple Gelatin

1 (3 ounce) package lime gelatin
1 cup water
1 (20 ounce) can sliced pineapple, drained

Prepare gelatin with 1 cup boiling water. Mix until well dissolved. Leaving pineapple slices in the can, pour gelatin over pineapple. Cover and chill until firm. To unmold, open can from bottom and push out onto a dish. Slice between pineapple slices and serve.

Watergate-Pistachio Salad

1 (20 ounce) can crushed pineapple, undrained
1 (12 ounce) carton frozen whipped topping, thawed
1 (3.4 ounce) package dry, instant, pistachio pudding mix

Combine and mix all ingredients. Spoon into a pretty glass serving dish. Chill 2 to 3 hours before serving.

Optional: You may add chopped nuts, maraschino cherries or miniature marshmallows.

Pineapple Boats

1 fresh pineapple
1 (15 ounce) can tropical fruit salad, drained
2 tablespoons shredded coconut

Cut fresh, whole pineapple in half (leaves and all). Remove core and fruit, leaving ½-inch thick shell. Chop pineapple and set aside. Fill with drained, tropical fruit, mixed with reserved pineapple. Sprinkle coconut over top.

Lox-Stuffed Celery

¼ pound lox, chopped
1 (8 ounce) package cream cheese, softened
4 ribs celery, cut in 2-inch sticks

Combine lox and cream cheese and beat until well blended. Spread mixture on celery.

Quick Ambrosia

1 (11 ounce) can mandarin oranges
1 (15¼ ounce) can pineapple chunks
2 tablespoons shredded coconut, divided

Drain oranges and pineapple. Combine and divide among 4 dessert dishes. Sprinkle each with 1 tablespoon coconut.

Fresh Fruit Medley

1 fresh pineapple
1 cup quartered, fresh strawberries
1 cup seedless grapes

Cut fresh, whole pineapple in half lengthwise. Cut out middle of pineapple and cut into chunks. Combine chunks, grapes and strawberries. Fill hollowed out pineapple boats with fruit. Serve chilled.

Martha Breckenridge's
Fresh Fruit Salad

2 cups halved, seedless, red and green grapes
2 cups cubed cantaloupe
2 cups sliced, fresh strawberries

Combine and mix all ingredients. Refrigerate until serving time. (You may top fruit salad with Strawberry Fruit Dip on page 82 if you have time.)

Desiree's Fruit Salad

1 (15 ounce) can chunky fruit salad, drained
2 bananas, sliced
1 cup red seedless grapes

Combine all ingredients; mixing well. Cover and refrigerate until ready to serve. (You may top this salad with Orange-Fruit Dip on page 45.)

Chunky Applesauce

3 cups chopped cooking apples
⅓ cup sugar
½ teaspoon cinnamon

Spread apples in a glass dish. Cover with vented, plastic wrap and microwave on high for 1 minute, then stir. Microwave 1 minute longer. Stir in sugar and microwave for 2 minutes, then stir. Sprinkle with cinnamon and serve.

Cranberry-Orange Relish

1 (16 ounce) can whole berry cranberries
⅔ cup orange marmalade
⅓ cup chopped walnuts

Combine all ingredients and mix well; cover and chill 2 to 3 hours before serving. Serve with pork or ham.

Optional: You may substitute ½ cup sliced maraschino cherries for walnuts.

Frozen Cranberry Salad

1 (16 ounce) can whole cranberry sauce
1 (8 ounce) carton frozen, whipped topping, thawed
1 (15 ounce) can crushed pineapple, drained

Combine all ingredients and mix well. Spoon into a 7 x 11-inch dish. Freeze.

Variation: Line muffin tin with paper cups; fill and freeze.

Jim Wornall's
Peach and Cottage Cheese Salad

1 cup cottage cheese
1 (15 ounce) can peach halves or slices, drained
Maraschino cherries

Place a scoop of cottage cheese in center of a salad plate, surrounded by peaches. Place a maraschino cherry on top of cottage cheese as a garnish. This is my husband's favorite salad.

Optional: You may place cottage cheese on a lettuce leaf.

Strawberry-Souffle Salad

1 (6 ounce) package strawberry gelatin
1 cup boiling water
2 cups mashed strawberries

Stir gelatin in the boiling water until dissolved. Add mashed berries and mix. Refrigerate until mixture begins to thicken, then whip with an electric mixer to a very stiff froth. Serve in sherbet dishes or small bowls.

Salad Dressing

1 (16 ounce) carton small curd cottage cheese
2 cups buttermilk
1 (2 ounce) package ranch-style salad dressing mix

Combine all ingredients in a bowl and mix well. Pour into a
1-quart covered container or jar and shake until blended.
Keep refrigerated. Shake before using. The dressing can be
poured into a blender and blended until smooth.

Judy Mueller's
Honey-Lime Dressing

¼ cup fresh lime juice
¼ cup honey
¼ teaspoon dijon mustard

Mix all ingredients together. Cover and refrigerate. Serve
chilled over lettuce or fruit salads. Judy serves this dressing
over a romaine and honeydew melon salad.

Judith's Walnut-Cranberry Relish

1 (16 ounce) can whole berry cranberries
1 (8 ounce) can crushed pineapple, drained
½ cup chopped walnuts

Combine all ingredients and mix well; chill.

Velora Holt's Cole Slaw Dressing

1 cup mayonnaise
½ cup sugar
¼ cup vinegar

Combine all ingredients and mix until well blended.
Refrigerate. Use dressing for cole slaw or waldorf salad.

Bean and Corn Salsa

½ cup canned black beans, drained
½ cup canned whole kernel corn, drained
1 cup thick and chunky salsa

Combine all ingredients in a small bowl and mix well. Keep
refrigerated. Serve with enchiladas or other Mexican food.

Spinach-Bacon Salad

2 quarts fresh spinach, torn into pieces
8 bacon slices, cooked, crumbled
3 eggs, hard-boiled, chopped

Toss all ingredients together.

Optional: You may toss with ranch-style dressing.

Summer Spinach Salad

4 cups fresh spinach, torn into pieces
12 fresh strawberries, sliced
1 cup halved, seedless grapes

Combine all ingredients.

Optional: You may substitute romaine lettuce for spinach. Toss and serve with poppy seed dressing.

Spinach-Orange Salad

2 cups spinach, torn into pieces
⅓ cup toasted, slivered almonds
1 (11 ounce) can mandarin oranges

Toss all ingredients together.

Optional: Toss with vinegar and oil dressing or poppy seed dressing.

Doris Hanks'
Tomato-Asparagus Salad

1 pound fresh asparagus spears
1 head romaine lettuce
2 fresh tomatoes, sliced

Cook fresh asparagus in boiling water for 5 to 6 minutes or steam until tender and drain. Chill asparagus. Line 4 salad plates with romaine lettuce leaves. Arrange chilled asparagus spears and tomato slices over the lettuce.

Optional: You may drizzle with Italian salad dressing.

Spinach, Apple and Walnut Salad

6 cups fresh spinach leaves, torn into pieces
2 red delicious apples, cored, chopped
½ cup coarsely chopped walnuts

Combine the ingredients in a salad bowl and toss until well mixed.

Optional: You may serve with poppy seed dressing.

Greek Summer Salad

4 cups fresh spinach, torn into pieces
1½ cups sliced strawberries
⅓ cup crumbled feta cheese

Combine and toss all ingredients. Cover and refrigerate until serving time.

Optional: You may serve with an oil and vinegar dressing.

Pepperoni Salad

2 cups iceberg lettuce, torn into pieces
½ cup pepperoni slices
½ cup shredded mozzarella cheese

Toss all ingredients together.

Optional: You may add sliced black olives and serve with Italian salad dressing.

Fruited Ham Toss

2 cups sliced, red delicious apples
4 cups mixed salad greens
1 (6 ounce) package sliced, cooked ham

Combine apples and salad greens. Cut ham into strips and toss with greens and apples.

Optional: You may serve with ranch-style dressing.

Shrimp and Spinach Salad

1 cup shrimp, cooked, drained
3 cups fresh spinach, torn into pieces
½ cup chopped celery

Combine, toss and serve.

Optional: If you'd like, Thousand Island dressing is great with this dish.

Crabmeat Salad

1 cup crabmeat, picked, flaked
1 cup chopped apples
¼ cup mayonnaise

Combine all ingredients, mixing well; chill. Serve on lettuce leaf.

Yield: 2 servings.

Optional: As a special touch, serve salad in avocado cups. Cut avocado in half, remove seed and fill hollow with crab salad.

Field Greens and Bacon Salad

1 (1 pound) package field greens
Tomato wedges or red onion rings
4 slices bacon

Combine greens and tomato wedges or red onion rings in bowl. Fry bacon on paper towels in microwave until crisp. Break into pieces and drain. Toss with greens.

Optional: You may use both tomatoes and onion rings. Serve with Ranch style dressing.

Romaine-Artichoke Salad

1 head romaine lettuce, torn into pieces
1 (13.75 ounce) can artichoke hearts, drained, chopped
1 large tomato, cut in wedges

Toss all ingredients together.

Optional: You may serve with French dressing.

Romaine and Melon Salad

2 cups romaine lettuce, cut into pieces
1 cup cubed honeydew melon
1 cup cubed cantaloupe

Toss lettuce and melon cubes in a salad bowl.

Optional: You may serve with Honey-Lime Dressing on page 85.

Boston Bibb Lettuce Salad

1 head bibb lettuce, torn into pieces
1 (11 ounce) can mandarin oranges, drained
⅓ cup chopped walnuts

Toss lettuce, oranges and walnuts.

Optional: You may serve with a poppy seed dressing.

Chicken Salad Veronique

2 cups cooked, sliced, chicken breasts
1 cup halved, seedless grapes
Mayonnaise

Combine chicken, grapes and just enough mayonnaise to moisten. Mix well and chill.

Cottage Cheese Salad

1 (24 ounce) carton cottage cheese, drained
⅓ cup chopped green onion
2 tomatoes, chopped

Combine all ingredients and mix well.

Optional: It is nice to serve this in large, red, hollowed out
tomatoes.

91

Carrot-Raisin Salad

6 carrots, scraped, shredded
1 cup raisins
½ cup mayonnaise

Combine all ingredients and mix well. Chill.

Willie Copeland's Cucumber Salad

2 cucumbers, sliced, peeled, seeded
½ cup sour cream
1 red onion, sliced

Combine all ingredients, mix and chill. (You may want to sprinkle some salt on the cucumbers.)

Greek Tomato Salad

3 ripe tomatoes, diced
½ cup crumbled feta cheese
½ teaspoon dried oregano

Arrange tomatoes on a serving plate. Sprinkle feta cheese over tomatoes and sprinkle with oregano.

Optional: You may serve with vinegar and oil dressing.

Stuffed-Tomato Salad

**4 tomatoes
1 (12 ounce) carton cottage cheese, drained
1 small onion, chopped**

Cut each tomato ¾ of the way down into 6 wedges; separate wedges slightly. Turn upside down and drain on napkins or cut off top of tomato and scoop out pulp, then drain. Combine cottage cheese and onion. Mix and fill tomato cavity.

Optional: You may stuff tomatoes with tuna salad instead of cottage cheese as a variation.

Tuna-Artichoke Salad

**2 (6 ounce) cans tuna fish
1 (13.75 ounce) can artichoke hearts, drained, chopped
Mayonnaise**

Drain tuna and flake. Combine and mix with artichoke hearts and enough mayonnaise to moisten.

Optional: You may add slivered almonds or substitute cooked, cubed, chicken breast or canned chicken for tuna.

Strawberry-Ginger Ale Salad

1 (6 ounce) package strawberry gelatin
1 cup ginger ale, chilled
1 (10 ounce) package frozen strawberries, thawed, chopped

Dissolve gelatin in 1 cup boiling water. Stir in 1 cup ginger ale. Refrigerate until partially thickened. Stir in strawberries. Mix well. Pour into a mold or square serving dish and chill until firm.

Optional: You may add sliced bananas or 1 (8 ounce) can crushed pineapple, drained.

Strawberry-Banana Whip

1 (3 ounce) package strawberry gelatin
1 (8 ounce) container frozen, whipped topping, thawed
2 bananas, sliced

Prepare gelatin with ¾ cup boiling water and stir until dissolved. Mix well. Chill until partially set. Whip gelatin, fold in whipped topping and blend. Stir in bananas and pour into a pretty glass bowl. Cover and chill until firm.

Optional: You may add chopped apples.

Instant Salad

1 (24 ounce) carton cottage cheese, drained
1 (6 ounce) package strawberry gelatin
1 (8 ounce) carton frozen, whipped topping, thawed

Combine drained, cottage cheese with dry gelatin and mix well. Fold in whipped topping. Spoon into a pretty glass serving dish. Refrigerate for 2 to 3 hours before serving.

Optional: You may stir in sliced strawberries.

Raspberry Sherbet Salad

1 (6 ounce) raspberry gelatin
1 pint raspberry sherbet
1 pint fresh or frozen raspberries

Dissolve gelatin in 1½ cups boiling water, mixing well, cool. Add sherbet and mix well. Refrigerate until partially set. Stir in berries; pour into 9 X 13-inch glass dish. Chill until set. Cut into squares.

Layered Raspberry-Cranberry Salad

2 (3 ounce) packages raspberry gelatin
1 (16 ounce) can whole berry cranberries
1 cup sour cream

Prepare gelatin with 1½ cups boiling water; chill until partially thickened. Stir in cranberries. Pour half the mixture in a dish and chill in freezer until firm. Spread sour cream over mixture. Top with remaining berry-gelatin mixture at room temperature. Chill until firm.

Anita McKee's Raspberry Salad

1 (6 ounce) package raspberry gelatin
1 (8 ounce) carton frozen, whipped topping, thawed
1 (10 ounce) package frozen,
unsweetened raspberries, thawed

Prepare gelatin with 1½ cups boiling water and mix well. Do not add any cold water. Cover and refrigerate until partially jelled. Beat with an electric mixer until fluffy. Fold in whipped topping and beat until blended. Stir in raspberries and spoon into a pretty serving bowl. Cover and refrigerate until firm.

Raspberry-Applesauce Salad

1 cup applesauce
1 (3 ounce) package raspberry gelatin
1 (10 ounce) package frozen raspberries, thawed

Heat applesauce just to boiling. Stir in dry gelatin and mix well. Stir in thawed raspberries. Pour into a mold or serving bowl and refrigerate until firm.

Margaret Sinclair's
Carrot-Pineapple Gelatin Salad

1 (3 ounce) box orange or lime gelatin
½ cup grated carrots
1 (8 ounce) can crushed pineapple, drained

Prepare gelatin with ¾ cup boiling water. Refrigerate until partially jelled. Stir in carrots and pineapple and pour into serving bowl. Chill for several hours before serving.

Wilma Davis'
Cinnamon Apple Salad

⅔ cup cinnamon, red hot candies
1 (3 ounce) package cherry gelatin
1½ cups applesauce

Heat cinnamon red hots in ⅔ cup boiling water until candy melts. Pour over dry gelatin and stir until well dissolved. Chill until partially set. Stir in applesauce and pour into a glass serving dish. Refrigerate until firm.

Shamrock Salad

1 (6 ounce) package lime gelatin
1 pint vanilla ice cream
2 bananas, sliced or 2 apples, chopped

Mix gelatin with 1½ cups boiling water. Cool. Stir in ice cream. Chill until partially set. Stir in sliced bananas or apples. Spoon into a glass serving dish. Chill until firm.

Lime-Applesauce Salad

1 (6 ounce) package lime gelatin
1 cup 7-Up
1 (16 ounce) can applesauce

Mix gelatin into 1 cup boiling water and stir until dissolved. Add 7-Up and mix well. Chill until partially set. Stir in applesauce. Pour into a 7x11-inch glass dish. Refrigerate until firm.

Wilma Davis' Cran-Apple Salad

1 (6 ounce) package orange gelatin
2 apples, peeled, chopped
1 (16 ounce) can whole berry cranberry sauce

Prepare gelatin, using 1 cup boiling water. Stir until well dissolved. Cool. Add apples and whole berry cranberry sauce, mixing well. Pour into a 7x11-inch glass dish. Cover and refrigerate until firm.

Lime-Gelatin Salad

1 (6 ounce) package lime gelatin
1 (15 ounce) can crushed pineapple, undrained
1 cup cottage cheese

Dissolve gelatin in 1 cup boiling water; chill until partially set. Stir in pineapple and cottage cheese. Pour into 7 x 11-inch glass dish. Refrigerate until firm; cut in squares to serve.

Optional: Add 1 banana, sliced.

Mandarin-Orange Whip

1 (3 ounce) box dry orange gelatin
1 (8 ounce) carton frozen, whipped topping
2 (11 ounce) cans mandarin oranges, drained

Combine the dry gelatin and whipped topping, mixing well. Stir in drained oranges; spoon into pretty, serving dish. Refrigerate for a couple of hours before serving.

Optional: Fold in 1 (8 ounce) can crushed pineapple, well drained.

Lime-Yogurt Salad

1 (8½ ounce) can pear halves, drained
2 (3 ounce) packages lime gelatin
1 (8 ounce) carton vanilla yogurt

Slice pears. Stir gelatin into 1½ cups boiling water until well dissolved. Divide gelatin into 2 bowls. Blend yogurt into 1 bowl of gelatin. In the other bowl, stir pears into remaining gelatin. Pour gelatin-yogurt mixture into a square, 9-inch dish and chill until partially thickened. Let pear mixture set. Pour gelatin-pear mixture onto the top of the chilled gelatin-yogurt mixture. Chill until firm. Cut into squares to serve.

Pam's Triple Orange Salad

1 (6 ounce) package orange gelatin
1 pint orange sherbet
1 (11 ounce) can mandarin oranges, drained

Dissolve gelatin with 1½ cups boiling water. Cool. Stir in sherbet, then oranges. Pour into serving dish. Refrigerate until firm.

Pam's Creamy Cranberry Mold

2 (3 ounce) packages cherry gelatin
1 (16 ounce) can jellied cranberry sauce
1 cup sour cream

Dissolve gelatin in 1¼ cups boiling water. Stir in cranberry sauce. Mix until well blended. Add sour cream and beat with an electric mixer until creamy. Pour into a mold and chill until firm.

Cherry-Cranberry Mold

1 (6 ounce) package cherry gelatin
1 (16 ounce) can whole cranberry sauce
1 (20 ounce) can cherry pie filling

Dissolve gelatin in 1 cup boiling water. Mix cranberries and cherry filling into gelatin. Pour into a mold or a 9 x 13-inch glass dish and refrigerate until firm.

Rogene's Cherry-Berry Salad

1 (6 ounce) package cherry gelatin
1 (10 ounce) package frozen strawberries, thawed
1 (16 ounce) can whole berry cranberry sauce

Dissolve gelatin in 1 cup boiling water; mix well. Stir in undrained strawberries and whole berry cranberry sauce, mixing well. Pour into 7x11-inch glass dish and refrigerate until set.

Optional: You may frost firm gelatin with sour cream.

Potato Soup

2 (10 ounce) cans potato soup
Cheddar cheese, shredded
Bacon, fried, drained, crumbled

Heat potato soup thoroughly. (You can mix 1 cup milk into soup, if desired.) Fry bacon until crisp; drain and crumble. Pour soup into soup bowls. Top with 1 or 2 tablespoons of cheddar cheese and desired amount of bacon.

Heidelberg Soup

2 (10½ ounce) cans potato soup
6 slices salami, cubed
10 green onions, chopped

Dilute soup according to directions. Saute cubed salami and onions in a well greased skillet. Add to soup and heat thoroughly. Serve hot.

Guacamole Soup

1 (18 ounce) can spicy V-8 tomato cocktail juice
½ cup chopped onion
2 avocados, peeled, seeded, chopped, divided

Heat V-8 juice and onion for 5 minutes or until very hot. Stir in ¾ of all the diced avocado and heat. Reserve ¼ of avocado for garnish. Sprinkle it on top of soup. Serve immediately.

Pat's Chilled Strawberry Soup

2 (10 ounce) packages strawberries in syrup
½ cup cranberries
2 (8 ounce) cartons strawberry yogurt

Combine all ingredients in blender and blend until smooth. Refrigerate 1 to 2 hours before serving. Serve chilled.

Quick Borscht

1 (15 ounce) jar tiny, whole red beets
1 (14½ ounce) can beef consomme
4 tablespoons sour cream

Drain and reserve beet liquid. Chop beets. Combine beets, liquid and the consomme in a saucepan and heat slowly for 10 minutes. Refrigerate until well chilled. Serve with a dollop of sour cream on top of each serving.

Tomato-Bacon Soup

1 (10 ounce) can tomato soup
1 (14 ½ ounce) can stewed tomatoes
with celery and peppers
4 strips bacon, fried, drained, crumbled

Combine soup and stewed tomatoes. Heat thoroughly. Sprinkle bacon over soup and serve hot.

Optional: You may add 1 can tomatoes and green chilies.

El Paso Tomato Soup

1 (10½ ounce) can tomato soup
1 (14½ ounce) can chopped stewed tomatoes with onion
1 (10 ounce) can chopped tomatoes and green chilies

Mix all ingredients plus 1 soup can water in a saucepan and heat to boiling, stirring often. Reduce heat and simmer for 5 minutes.

Steak Soup

**1 pound ground sirloin steak
2 (24 ounce) jars Simply Home Country Vegetable soup
1 (10 ounce) can tomatoes and green chilies**

In a skillet, brown ground sirloin. Crumble and drain. Stir in soups and tomatoes with juice. Heat on medium low heat, stirring often for 15 to 20 minutes or until hot.

Senate Bean Soup

**2 cups dried navy beans
6 cups water
½ pound ham hocks**

Soak beans, covered in water, overnight. Drain and pour beans in 6 cups water and cook with ham hocks for 2 to 3 hours or until tender. Season with salt and pepper.

Pinto Bean Soup

**2 (1 pound) packages dry pinto beans
1 smoked ham hock or 2 cups chopped ham
Salt to taste**

Wash beans. Cover with cold water and soak overnight. Drain and cover beans with water. Bring to a boil. Add ham. Reduce heat and simmer slowly 3 to 4 hours. You may need to add more water. When beans are tender, remove 2 to 3 cups of the beans and smash with potato masher. Return to pot. Season with salt.

Microwave Mushroom Soup

1 (10½ ounce) can cream of mushroom soup
1 (10½ ounce) can beef consomme
1 (4 ounce) can sliced mushrooms

Combine mushroom soup and consomme in a 2-quart bowl, mixing well. Microwave on high for 1 minute and stir. Add the can of sliced mushrooms and mix. Reduce heat to medium and microwave 1 minute longer or until hot. Stir before serving.

Mushroom Soup

1 (10¾ ounce) can cream of mushroom soup
1 (14½ ounce) can beef consomme
1 (4 ounce) can sliced beef

Combine all ingredients in a medium saucepan. Mix well and heat thoroughly. Yield: 4 servings.

Steve Kirk's Corn Soup

2 (15 ounce) cans whole kernel corn, undrained
3 tablespoons chunky salsa or to taste
2 tablespoons peach preserves or to taste

Combine all ingredients with 1 cup water and mix well. Bring to boil. Reduce heat and simmer 5 minutes.

3-Can Clam Chowder

1 (10½ ounce) can New England clam chowder
1 (10½ ounce) can cream of celery soup
1 (10½ ounce) can cream of potato soup

Combine all ingredients in saucepan and mix well. Heat thoroughly and serve.

Optional: You may dilute with 1 soup can of milk.

Sausage and Corn Chowder

¼ pound hot Italian sausage
1 (11 ounce) can Mexicorn
3 cups chicken broth

Remove casing from sausage. Place in a skillet and crumble. Cook over medium heat until meat is done. Stir in undrained corn and chicken broth. Mix well and simmer for 10 minutes or until hot.

Minute Stew

1 pound extra lean, ground meat
1 (15 ounce) can stewed tomatoes with onions
1 (8 ounce) can whole kernel corn, drained

Brown ground meat in skillet and drain. Add tomatoes and corn to skillet and mix well. Simmer for 20 to 30 minutes, stirring often.

Optional: You may add 1 (15 ounce) can small new potatoes.

Notes

106

Side Dishes
& Veggies

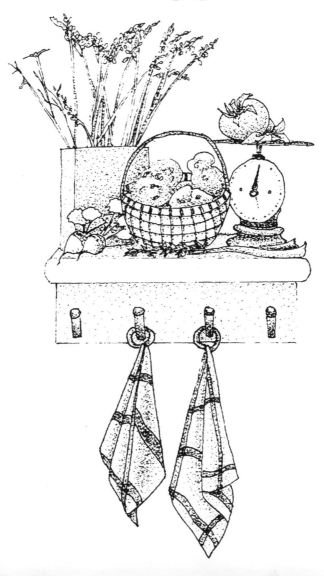

Charlotte's Onion-Roasted Potatoes

2 pounds potatoes
1 (1 ounce) envelope dry onion soup mix
⅓ cup olive oil

Wash and peel potatoes. Cut into chunks. Pour all ingredients into a large plastic bag, close bag and shake until potatoes are coated. Empty potatoes into a greased 9 x 13-inch pan. Bake at 450° for 40 minutes or until tender and golden brown, stirring occasionally.

Dilled New Potatoes

24 small, red skinned potatoes
4 tablespoons fresh dill, chopped
4 tablespoons margarine, melted

Boil potatoes until tender and drain. Slice, mix dill and margarine and toss with potatoes. Serve hot.

Microwave Potato Skins

4 baked potatoes
1 cup shredded cheddar cheese
4-6 slices bacon, fried crisp, drained, crumbled

Slice potatoes lengthwise and microwave for 3 minutes. Scoop out potato, leaving ¼-inch potato on skins. Fill each potato skin with cheese and bacon. Place on plate. Cover with paper towel or plastic wrap and microwave for 30 seconds or until cheese is melted. Yield: 4 servings of 2 potato skins per person.

Nacho Potato Wedges

3 medium potatoes, cut into wedges
1 cup Velveeta cheese, cubed
1 cup jalapeno peppers

Bake potatoes at 400° for 30 minutes or until golden brown or deep fry and drain. Melt cheese in the microwave for 1 minute on high. Stir and cook until cheese melts. Stir until smooth. Pour over potatoes. Dot each potato wedge with 1 or 2 jalapeno slices.

Rosemary-Roasted Potatoes

2 pounds new, red potatoes
3 tablespoons olive oil
2 tablespoons crushed, dried, rosemary leaves

Wash potatoes. Peel a narrow strip around centers. Place potatoes in a greased, 9 x 13-inch pan. Drizzle with olive oil and sprinkle with rosemary. Stir to coat. Bake uncovered at 350° for 1 hour and 15 minutes or until skins are crispy and potatoes are fork-tender.

Skinny Mashed Potatoes

5 large potatoes, cut in 1-inch pieces
3½ cups chicken broth, divided
½ teaspoon white pepper or to taste

Place potatoes and 2¼ cups broth in large saucepan. Heat to boil on high, then reduce to medium. Cover and cook 10 minutes or until potatoes are tender. Drain, but reserve broth. Mash potatoes with 1¼ cups broth and pepper until desired consistency is reached, adding more broth, if needed.

Note: You may use black pepper if you don't mind the little black specs.

Pizza Potatoes

1 (5.5 ounce) box scalloped potatoes
1 cup shredded mozzarella cheese
1 cup pepperoni slices

Prepare potatoes according to package directions, but do not bake. Pour into a greased casserole dish. Spread cheese over potatoes and arrange pepperoni slices over cheese. Cover and bake at 400° for 30 to 35 minutes.

Gay Herndon's Potato Casserole

5 potatoes, peeled, sliced
1 (10½ ounce) can golden cream of mushroom soup
1 cup grated cheddar cheese

Place sliced potatoes in a greased, 2-quart casserole dish. Dilute soup with ½ cup milk or water and mix well. Pour over the potatoes. Bake covered at 400° for 45 minutes covered. Uncover and top with cheese and bake 15 minutes longer.

Optional: You may add 1 chopped onion before baking.

Caviar Potatoes

4 baking potatoes
1 (8 ounce) carton sour cream
1 (2 ounce) jar caviar

Bake potatoes at 400° for 1 hour or until done. Split potatoes lengthwise and serve with a dollop of sour cream. Top with a spoonful of caviar.

Boiled New Potatoes

3 pounds small, new potatoes
1½ sticks margarine, melted
6 tablespoons minced parsley

Cook small, new potatoes in 5 cups boiling water until tender and drain. Sprinkle with melted margarine and minced parsley. Serve hot.

Jessica Wornall's
Southwestern Baked Potatoes

4 baking potatoes
1 (8 ounce) jar thick and chunky salsa
4 tablespoons shredded cheddar cheese

Wash potatoes and prick their skins several times. Bake at 400° for 1 hour or until tender. (Do not wrap potatoes in foil.) Split potatoes lengthwise. Squeeze potatoes or scratch with a fork so that the salsa will soak into the potato. Spoon desired amount of salsa into each potato. Top with shredded cheese.

Baked Onion French Fries

1 (1 ounce) envelope dry onion soup mix
3 teaspoons canola oil
1 (24 ounce) package French fried potatoes

In a large bowl, combine soup mix and oil. Add potatoes and stir until coated with soup mixture. Bake according to directions on potatoes, stirring as needed.

Glazed Sweet Potatoes

4 sweet potatoes
½ cup packed brown sugar
¼ cup melted margarine

Pierce potatoes several times with a fork. Microwave on high for 10 minutes or until fork tender and cool. Peel and slice potatoes and place in a greased, baking dish. Sprinkle brown sugar over potatoes and top with margarine. Cover and microwave on high for 4 minutes then stir. Microwave for 1 or 2 minutes longer. Let stand covered for 3 minutes before serving.

112

Orange Sweet Potatoes

1 (18 ounce) can sweet potatoes, drained
¼ teaspoon salt
⅓ cup orange marmalade

Place sweet potatoes sprinkled with salt in a casserole dish and cover. Microwave on high for 4 minutes and stir. Spoon marmalade over potatoes. Cover and microwave for 1 or 2 minutes longer or until hot. Stir before serving.

Seasoned Pasta

2 (14.5 ounce) cans seasoned chicken broth
with Italian herbs
3 cups uncooked, corkscrew pasta
½ to 1 cup grated parmesan cheese

Heat broth in a saucepan until it boil. Stir in uncooked pasta. Reduce heat and simmer on medium until pasta is fork tender, stirring often. Pour into a serving bowl and sprinkle with parmesan cheese.

Desiree Wornall's
Baked Macaroni and Cheese

1 (8 ounce) package macaroni
2⅓ cups milk
1 (8 ounce) carton Velveeta cheese, cubed

Cook macaroni according to package directions and drain. Stir in milk and cheese. Mix well. Pour into a greased, baking dish and bake covered at 350° for about 1 hour or until set.

113

Macaroni and Cheese

1 (16 ounce) package macaroni, divided
1 (12 ounce) package shredded cheddar cheese, divided
1 (16 ounce) can whole tomatoes,
drained, chopped, reserve juice, divided

Cook macaroni according to package directions. In a greased, 2-quart casserole, make alternating layers of half macaroni, half cheese and half tomatoes. Repeat layers. Pour reserved tomato juice over top. Bake covered at 350° for 1 hour.

Carole's Easy Dressing

1 (6 ounce) box cornbread stuffing mix
1 onion, chopped
1 (14 ounce) can chicken broth

Combine stuffing mix, contents of seasoning packet, onion and the broth in a bowl and mix well. Spray a baking dish with a nonstick cooking spray. Pour dressing into prepared dish and bake at 325° for 30 minutes.

Optional: You may add ½ cups chopped celery to dressing before baking.

Sausage Dressing

1 (6 ounce) box herb stuffing mix
1 pound bulk pork sausage
1 cup chopped onion

Prepare stuffing according to package directions. Brown and drain sausage. Remove sausage from skillet and saute onion in the drippings. Combine dressing, sausage and onions; mix well. Pour into a greased casserole dish and bake at 325° for 30 minutes.

Brown Rice

1 (14 ounce) can chicken broth
1 cup uncooked brown rice
1 teaspoon dried parsley

Bring broth to a boil over high heat in a heavy saucepan. Add rice, stir, cover and reduce heat to low so that rice simmers. Cook 50 minutes or until tender and broth is absorbed. Uncover and let rice set for 3 minutes. Fluff with a fork.

Optional: You may add ½ cup chopped onions and ½ cup chopped celery. Cook with the rice.

Rice Pilaf

2 cups cooked rice
⅓ cup raisins or chopped dates
¼ cup slivered almonds, toasted

Combine all ingredients and mix well. This rice is great with chicken.

Sausage-Rice Casserole

1 pound pork sausage
3 cups cooked rice
1 (10½ ounce) can golden cream of mushroom soup

Fry sausage, crumble and drain. Combine sausage, rice and mushroom soup and mix well. Pour into a greased casserole dish and bake at 350° for 30 minutes.

Pecan-Rice Pilaf

½ cup pecan halves
3 tablespoons margarine, melted
1 (6.7 ounce) package wild rice

Saute pecan halves in melted margarine. Prepare wild rice according to package directions. Stir pecans into rice. Serve hot with chicken or pork.

Long Grain and
Wild Rice Almondine

1 (6.7 ounce) package long grain and wild rice
3 tablespoon butter
¼ cup sliced almonds

Prepare rice according to package directions. Heat butter and saute almonds. Stir buttered almonds into hot cooked rice.

Hopping John

**1 cup long grain rice
1 onion, chopped
2 (15 ounce) cans black-eyed peas**

Cook rice with 2 cups boiling, salted water according to package directions. Saute onion in 3 tablespoons margarine. Add onion to black-eyed peas. Serve rice with peas on top.

Optional: Add 1 cup cooked, chopped ham to peas.

Deviled Eggs

**6 hard-boiled eggs, halved
Thousand Island salad dressing
Paprika**

Slice eggs lengthwise; remove yolks. Chop yolks and mix with enough dressing to moisten. Stuff into egg white shells. Sprinkle with paprika. Refrigerate.

Fried Bananas

**3 to 4 very firm bananas
Brown sugar
Peanut oil**

Slice bananas and sprinkle with brown sugar. Fry in hot peanut oil until bananas are light brown and crisp. Drain. Serve immediately.

Glazed Pineapple Slices

1 (20 ounce) can pineapple slices, drained
2 tablespoons butter
3 tablespoons brown sugar

Arrange pineapple slices in a large, microwave dish. Brush with melted butter. Sprinkle with brown sugar. Microwave on high for 1 to 2 minutes or until butter and sugar glaze is bubbly. Serve hot with ham or pork.

Broccoli Casserole

1 (10 ounce) package frozen, broccoli florets, thawed
1 (10¾ ounce) can cream of celery soup
½ cup shredded cheddar cheese

Cook broccoli according to package directions. Drain. Spread in bottom of greased baking dish. Cover with celery soup. Sprinkle cheese over the top. Bake at 350° for 20 to 25 minutes or until hot.

Barbara Wright's Lemon Broccoli

1 (10 ounce) package frozen broccoli, thawed
2 tablespoons margarine
1½ tablespoons lemon juice

Prepare broccoli according to package directions; drain. Melt margarine and remove from heat. Stir in lemon juice. Mix together, then pour over broccoli.

Broccoli-Rice Casserole

1 (10 ounce) box frozen chopped broccoli, thawed
1 cup cooked rice
1 (8 ounce) jar Cheez Whiz

Cook broccoli according to package directions and drain.
Cook rice according to package directions. Combine
broccoli, rice and Cheez Whiz and mix well. Pour into
greased dish and bake at 350° for 20 to 30 minutes.

Orange Broccoli

1½ pounds fresh broccoli
¼ cup margarine or butter, melted
3 tablespoons orange juice

Trim broccoli and discard some of the stems. Steam covered
for 8 to 10 minutes or until tender. Place in a serving bowl.
Mix margarine and orange juice in a small bowl and pour
over broccoli.

Cabbage Casserole

1 head cabbage, cut up, cooked, drained
1 (10½ ounce) can cream of chicken soup
1 cup shredded cheddar cheese

In a buttered baking dish, make alternate layers of cabbage,
soup and cheese. Repeat layers. Bake at 350° for 30
minutes.

Maxine McNeil's Orange Carrots

1 tablespoon butter or margarine
2 tablespoon orange marmalade
1 (15 ounce) can sliced carrots, drained

Combine butter and marmalade in saucepan and heat until melted, stirring often. Add drained carrots. Stir and heat until hot and glazed.

Ritzy Carrot Casserole

2 (15 ounce) cans carrots, drained
1 (8 ounce) jar Cheese Whiz
1 tube Ritz crackers, crushed

Heat carrots and pour into a greased baking dish. Heat Cheese Whiz and pour over carrots. Sprinkle cracker crumbs on top. Bake at 300° for 30 minutes or until golden brown.

Velma Stewart's Stuffed Celery

4 ribs celery
1 (8 ounce) package cream cheese, softened
16 pimento-stuffed green olives, sliced

Cut celery into 2-inch lengths. Stuff with cream cheese. Dot with green olive slices.

Optional: You may sprinkle with paprika instead of using green olives.

Creamed Corn

2 (10 ounce) boxes frozen whole kernel corn
1 (8 ounce) package cream cheese, softened
Lemon pepper to taste

Cook corn according to package directions and drain. Stir cream cheese into hot corn. Stir until heated thoroughly. Season to taste with lemon pepper.

Mexican Corn

1 (16 ounce) package frozen corn, thawed
½ cup thick and chunky salsa
¼ cup sliced ripe olives

Cook corn according to package directions. Stir in salsa and olives. Cook until hot. Drain.

Baked Corn On The Cob

6 ears fresh corn
6 tablespoons margarine
1 teaspoon lemon pepper

Husk fresh corn and remove silk. Wash and dry with paper towels. Spread margarine on corn, sprinkle with lemon pepper and wrap in foil. Bake at 325° for 30 minutes.

Yield: 6 servings.

Company Cauliflower

1 head cauliflower, divided
1 cup sour cream, divided
1 cup shredded cheddar cheese, divided

Rinse cauliflower and separate into flowerets. Cook in a 2-quart, covered saucepan in 1-inch boiling, salted water for 8 to 10 minutes or until tender. Drain well. Place half cauliflower in a greased, casserole dish. Spread ½ cup sour cream over cauliflower. Sprinkle with ½ cup cheese. Repeat layers. Bake at 325° 20 minutes or until hot and cheese has melted.

Cauliflower and Green Peas

1 (10 ounce) package frozen cauliflower, thawed
1 (15 ounce) can green peas, drained
3 tablespoons margarine

Prepare cauliflower according to package directions and drain. Stir in green peas and margarine. Heat thoroughly, stirring occasionally.

Optional: You may saute 1 cup chopped celery and add to the cauliflower and peas.

Lila Obercrom's
Green Beans and Bacon

6 slices bacon
1 cup chopped onion
2 pounds fresh green beans
or 2 (14.5 ounce) cans green beans

Fry bacon until crisp; drain on paper towels. Cook onions in bacon drippings until slightly wilted and stir in beans. Cook 1 minute. If you are cooking fresh green beans, add 1 tablespoon water, cover and cook 3 minutes. Uncover and cook 10 minutes longer. If you are using the canned green beans, the 4 minute cooking time is enough. Crumble bacon and add just before serving.

Green Beans and Ham

¼ cup chopped onion
2 (15 ounce) cans green beans, drained
½ cup chopped, baked ham

Saute onion in margarine, combine all ingredients in a saucepan and heat 5 minutes. Stir as needed. Serve hot.

Green Bean Casserole

2 (15 ounce) cans green beans, drained
1 (10¾ ounce) can cream of celery soup
1 cup crushed potato chips

Combine green beans and soup. Pour into a greased, 2-quart casserole dish. Top with crushed potato chips. Bake at 350° for 25 to 30 minutes.

Audrey's Green Beans

1 (15 ounce) can cut green beans, undrained
1 teaspoon olive oil
1 tablespoon dry onion soup mix

Combine all ingredients in a saucepan. Mix and heat thoroughly.

Hint: You must use olive oil for the best taste.

Basil Green Beans

1 (10 ounce) package frozen, French-style green beans
2 tablespoons butter or margarine
½ teaspoon dried basil

Combine all ingredients in a saucepan. Cover and bring to a boil. Reduce heat and simmer until all liquid is gone, stirring as needed.

Green Beans Almondine

2 (10 ounce) packages frozen green beans, thawed
⅓ cup slivered almonds
3 tablespoons margarine, melted

Cook beans according to package directions and drain well. In a small saucepan saute almonds in melted margarine. Stir almonds and margarine into green beans.

Men's Favorite Green Beans

2 (15 ounce) cans green beans, drained
2 tablespoons pimento, finely chopped
1 (8 ounce) jar Cheez Whiz

Combine all ingredients and mix well; heat thoroughly.

Myrtle Hull's Green Bean Casserole

2 (15 ounce) can green beans, drained
1 (10½ ounce) can cream of mushroom soup
1 (2.8 ounce) can fried onion rings, divided

Combine beans, soup and half of onion rings and mix well.
Pour into a greased, baking dish and bake at 350° for 25
minutes. Top with remaining onion rings and bake 10
minutes longer.

Green Peas Casserole

2 (10 ounce) packages frozen green peas
1 cup shredded cheddar cheese
1 (10¾ ounce) can golden mushroom soup

Cook peas according to package directions and drain.
Combine peas, cheese and soup. Bake in a greased
casserole dish at 350° for 30 to 35 minutes.

Optional: You may top casserole with ½ cup seasoned
breadcrumbs before baking.

Minted Peas

1 (15 ounce) can green peas, reserve liquid
1 tablespoon margarine
⅓ cup mint jelly

Cook liquid from green peas until it has reduced to ¼ cup. Stir in peas, margarine and mint jelly. Heat thoroughly.

Cheesy Green Peas

2 (15 ounce) cans green peas, undrained
3 tablespoons chopped onion
1 (8 ounce) jar Cheez Whiz

Combine peas, onions and cheese. Mix well and heat thoroughly in microwave or bake at 325 ° for 15 minutes.

Optional: To spice up the peas, you may use jalapeno Cheez Whiz instead of regular Cheez Whiz.

Green Peas Deluxe

2 (10 ounce) packages frozen green peas, thawed
1 (8 ounce) can chopped water chestnuts, drained
1 (10½ ounce) can golden cream of mushroom soup

Prepare green peas according to package directions and drain. Stir in water chestnuts and soup. Heat well in a saucepan or pour into a greased baking dish and bake at 350° for 25 minutes.

Snow Peas

1½ pounds fresh snow peas
1 tablespoon lemon juice
3 tablespoons margarine

Steam peas in a steamer for 3 to 4 minutes. Season with lemon juice and margarine.   Add salt to taste.

Vegetable Casserole

1 onion, chopped
2 (15 ounce) cans peas and carrots, drained
1 (8 ounce) package Velveeta cheese, cubed

Saute onion in 2 tablespoons margarine. Combine all ingredients and pour into a 2-quart baking dish. Bake at 350° for 25 to 30 minutes.

Hominy Casserole

2 (15½ ounce) cans yellow hominy, drained
1 small onion, chopped
1 cup shredded cheddar cheese

Place alternate layers of hominy, onion and cheese in a greased baking dish. Repeat layers. Bake at 350° for 30 minutes.

Deluxe Asparagus

1 (15 ounce) can cut asparagus
2 eggs, beaten
¾ cup shredded, Mexican-style 3-cheese blend

Drain asparagus and reserve 4 tablespoons liquid. In a bowl, combine eggs and reserved asparagus liquid, mixing well. Arrange asparagus in a greased, baking dish. Pour egg mixture over asparagus. Sprinkle cheese over top. Bake at 350° for 30 minutes.

Optional: You may sprinkle ¼ cup sliced almonds over cheese.

Fried Onion Rings

2 onions, sliced
1 cup pancake mix
Enough water or milk to make a batter

Separate sliced onions into rings. Mix together pancake mix and water (or milk if directions call for it). Dip onion rings into batter. Fry in deep oil until golden brown. Drain on paper towels.

Mother's Fried Green Tomatoes

2 green tomatoes, sliced
½ cup flour or cornmeal
Vegetable oil

Dip tomato slices in flour or cornmeal. Fry in vegetable oil until golden brown.

Julie's Scalloped Onions

6 onions, peeled, sliced
½ (16 ounce) box Velveeta cheese, sliced
3 cups crushed potato chips

Boil onions until limp and transparent. Butter a casserole dish and layer onions alternately with cheese and potato chips. Repeat layers. Bake at 350° for 20 minutes.

Onion-Rice Casserole

1 (10½ ounce) can French onion soup
1 cup regular rice
½ cup chopped celery

Combine soup, rice, celery and 1 cup water. Mix well and cook in a covered saucepan over medium heat for 25 to 30 minutes or until the rice is tender. Fluff with a fork.

Vidalia Onions

4 Vidalia onions or sweet onions
4 teaspoons butter
4 teaspoons chicken bouillon granules

Peel onions. Use spoon to "hollow out" top of onions. Spoon butter and bouillon into each cavity. Place on a microwave plate and heat on high for 1½ minutes or until fork-tender.

129

New Year's Black-Eyed Peas

1 (15 ounce) can black-eyed peas, drained
8 slices pepperoni, chopped
2 tablespoons chopped onion

Combine peas, pepperoni and onion. Heat thoroughly.

Everyone who eats black-eyed peas on New Year's Day
will have good luck in the New Year!

Refried Beans and Cheese

1 (15 ounce) can refried beans
⅓ cup shredded cheddar cheese
1 to 2 tablespoons chopped, green onions

Spoon beans into a microwave dish and microwave for 2
minutes. Sprinkle cheese over top of beans and microwave
until cheese melts. Before serving, sprinkle chopped green
onions over beans. Serve as a vegetable or as a dip with
tortilla chips.

Speedy Baked Beans

3 (15 ounce) cans pork and beans
6 tablespoons chili sauce
⅓ cup packed brown sugar

Mix the beans, chili sauce and sugar. Bake uncovered in a
greased casserole dish at 325° for 1 hour.

Optional: You may also lay 3 or 4 strips of bacon on top of beans
before baking for added flavor.

Creamed Spinach

1 (10 ounce) package frozen, chopped spinach, thawed
1 (10½ ounce) can cream of mushroom soup
½ teaspoon nutmeg

Cook spinach according to package directions and drain well. Combine spinach and soup, mixing well. Simmer for 10 to 15 minutes, stirring occasionally. Sprinkle with nutmeg.

Zucchini Casserole

4 zucchini, chopped
1 tube Ritz crackers, crushed
1 (8 ounce) jar Cheez Whiz, melted

Cook zucchini in small amount of water until tender and drain. Alternate layers of zucchini and crushed crackers in a greased, casserole dish. Pour melted cheese over zucchini and crackers. Bake at 350° for 30 minutes.

Optional: You may add 2 chopped yellow squash and cook with zucchini.

Zucchini Rounds

½ cup baking mix
2 beaten eggs
2 cups raw, grated, unpeeled zucchini

Combine baking mix and eggs, mixing well. Stir in grated zucchini. Fry as you would pancakes, dropping spoonfuls of batter onto a hot, greased griddle. Drain and serve hot.

Baked Acorn Squash

3 acorn squash, halved
1½ sticks butter
6 tablespoons brown sugar

Cut squash in half. Remove seeds and pulp. Put 2 tablespoons butter into each half. Sprinkle 1 tablespoon brown sugar in each. Place in a large shallow pan and bake at 350° for 1 hour. Pour a little water in bottom of pan for simmering.

Myrtle Hull's White Sauce

4 tablespoons butter
4 tablespoons flour
2 cups milk

Melt butter in saucepan. Add flour and mix well. Remove from heat. Gradually stir in milk and return to heat. Cook, stirring constantly, until thickened and smooth. Serve over vegetables.

Cheese Sauce

1 (10 ½ ounce) can cream of mushroom soup
1 (8 ounce) carton sour cream
1 cup shredded cheddar cheese

In a saucepan, combine all ingredients and mix well. Heat on medium until hot, but do not boil. Serve over vegetables or fish.

Vegetable Christmas Tree

1 head broccoli
1 head cauliflower
24 cherry tomatoes

Build the tree on a large tray or platter. Make the tree trunk out of the broccoli stem. Build the first row of the tree with cauliflowerets, next row with tomatoes, alternating rows. Decrease size of each row. Outline tree with broccoli flowerets. Serve with dip of choice.

Notes

Main dishes

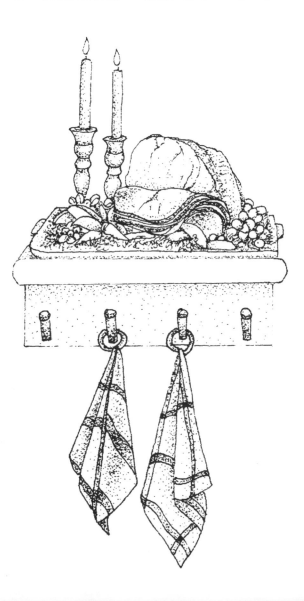

Artichoke Chicken

8 boneless, skinless chicken breasts
1 (6½ ounce) jar marinated artichoke hearts
8 slices Swiss cheese

Between 2 pieces of waxed paper, flatten chicken to uniform thickness. Brown chicken breasts on both sides in a well greased skillet. Arrange chicken in a single layer in a greased, 9 x 13-inch pan. Drain artichoke hearts and chop coarsely. Spread on top of chicken. Lay Swiss cheese over all and bake at 350° for 25 to 40 minutes until chicken is tender and cheese melts.

Chicken Cacciatore

4 boneless, skinless chicken breasts
2 cups chunky spaghetti sauce with onions
1 green pepper, cored, seeded, cut in strips

Brown chicken in a well greased skillet, turning frequently to brown all sides; drain. Add spaghetti sauce and green peppers to chicken. Cover skillet and cook on low for 35 minutes or until chicken is tender. To serve, place chicken on a platter. Pour tomato-pepper mixture over chicken.

Optional: You may sprinkle with parmesan cheese.

Honey-Orange Glazed Chicken

4 boneless, skinless, chicken breasts
¼ cup honey
⅓ cup orange marmalade

Place chicken in a 7 x 11-inch baking dish. Set aside. Combine honey and marmalade in a small bowl. Microwave uncovered for 1 minute or until glaze is melted and hot. Stir. Spread half of mixture over chicken. Cover and bake at 350º for 45 minutes. Uncover and cook another 10 minutes with remaining glaze or until chicken is lightly browned.

Jane Ballard's Cajun Chicken

4 boneless, skinless, chicken breast halves
1 teaspoon Tabasco sauce
1 teaspoon Cajun seasoning

Rinse chicken in cool water and dry. Generously sprinkle Tabasco sauce on each side, then season each side with Cajun seasoning. Spray skillet with a nonstick cooking spray. Place chicken in skillet and brown. Turn and brown other side. Cover and cook slowly, about 20 minutes until fork tender.

Penny Sparks' Chicken and Noodles

4 chicken breasts, cubed, boiled
1 (8 ounce) package egg noodles
2 (10½ ounce) cans cream of mushroom soup

In a saucepan, cover chicken with water and boil until tender. Add more water if needed and add egg noodles and cook until tender. Drain. Stir in cream of mushroom soup and heat thoroughly.

137

Chicken Dijon

6 boneless, skinless chicken breasts
4 tablespoons dijon mustard
2 cups finely crumbled, seasoned breadcrumbs

Place chicken breasts in a greased baking dish and bake at 350° for 20 minutes. Remove from heat. Generously spread mustard on both sides of chicken, then coat with breadcrumbs and return to baking dish. Bake at 350° for 1 hour. The mustard gives the chicken a tangy flavor and makes it moist.

Honey Mustard Chicken Tenders

1 pound boneless, skinless chicken tenders
3½ tablespoons honey mustard
1⅓ cups French fried onions, crushed

Coat chicken with mustard. Roll in crushed onions. Place on a greased baking pan. Bake at 400° for 15 minutes or until chicken is done.

Bev West's
Cranberry Sauce For Chicken

1 (15 ounce) can whole berry cranberry sauce
1 (1 ounce) envelope dry onion soup mix
1 (8 ounce) bottle French dressing

Combine the 3 ingredients in a bowl and mix until well blended. Cover and refrigerate until ready to use.

Bev West's Cranberry Chicken

8 boneless, skinless, chicken breast halves
Bev West's Cranberry Sauce For Chicken
Salt

Place 8 boneless, skinless, chicken breast halves in a glass dish and pour Cranberry Sauce evenly over chicken. Cover and marinate overnight in the refrigerator. The next day, bake at 350° for 1 hour or until tender.

Note: This may not sound great, but tastes delicious. It will surprise you.

Mary Alice Lawrence's
Baked Chicken and Rice Casserole

1 (6 ounce) box long grain and wild rice
6 boneless, skinless chicken breasts
1 (10 ½ ounce) can cream of mushroom soup

In a greased 2½-quart baking dish, mix box of rice, seasoning packet and 2 cups hot water. Place chicken on top of rice. Bake covered at 350° for 1½ hours. Dilute mushroom soup with ½ cup water; mix and then pour over the chicken. Bake uncovered for 20 minutes or until soup bubbles and chicken is brown.

Velma Stewart's Russian Chicken Sauce

1 (8 ounce) bottle Russian salad dressing
1 (8 ounce) jar apricot preserves
1 (1 ounce) envelope dry onion soup mix

Combine Russian dressing, dry soup mix and apricot preserves and mix well.

Velma Stewart's Russian Chicken

6 boneless, skinless, chicken breasts
Velma Stewart's Russian Chicken Sauce
Salt

Pour Velma Stewart's Russian Chicken Sauce over chicken in a buttered 9 x 13-inch dish. Bake at 300° for 2 hours.

Onion Chicken

4 to 6 boneless, skinless chicken breasts
1 (1 ounce) envelope dry onion soup mix
2 tablespoons margarine, melted

Trim off all visible fat. Place chicken breasts in a sprayed 9 x 13-inch baking dish. Sprinkle onion soup mix and melted margarine over chicken. Cover and bake at 350° for 1 hour.

Ernie Massey's Italian Chicken

6 boneless, skinless chicken breasts
½ cup flour
1 (8 ounce) bottle Italian salad dressing

Remove any fat from chicken. Roll chicken breasts in flour. Place in a greased 9 x 13-inch pan. Pour Italian dressing over chicken. Cover and bake at 350° for an hour or until tender. Remove, cover and bake until golden brown. This could be prepared in a slow cooker on low.

Chicken Mozzarella

6 boneless, skinless chicken breasts
½ (28 ounce) jar spaghetti sauce
6 slices mozzarella cheese

Place chicken breasts in a greased baking dish. Cover with sauce. Bake covered at 350° for 1 hour. Remove from oven. Top each breast with 1 slice cheese. Return to oven and bake uncovered for 10 minutes longer. Serve with spaghetti or noodles, if desired.

Betty Jo's Mushroom Chicken

4 boneless, skinless chicken breasts
1 (10½ ounce) can cream of mushroom soup
1 cup sour cream

Place chicken in a sprayed 9 x 13-inch baking pan. Combine mushroom soup and sour cream and pour over chicken. Bake at 350° for 1 hour or until fork tender.

Baked Mexican Chicken

4 to 6 boneless, skinless chicken breasts
1 teaspoon taco seasoning mix
1 (10 ounce) can enchilada sauce

Place chicken in a pan that has been sprayed with a nonstick cooking spray. Sprinkle desired amount of taco seasoning mix over chicken. Pour enchilada sauce over chicken. Bake at 350° for 1 hour or until tender. Serve with warmed corn tortillas.

Donna Spencer's Lemon Pepper Chicken

4 boneless, skinless chicken breasts
4 tablespoons soy sauce
1 teaspoon lemon pepper

Arrange chicken breasts in a greased, 9 x 13-inch pan. Sprinkle soy sauce and lemon pepper over chicken. Bake at 350° for 1 hour or until tender.

Lemon-Lime Chicken Breasts

4 boneless, skinless chicken breasts
⅓ cup lime juice
Lemon pepper

Pour lime juice over chicken and marinate for 30 minutes in refrigerator. Place chicken in a glass, pie plate. Cover with plastic wrap and prick a couple of holes in plastic with a fork. Microwave at full power for 8 minutes. Turn. Rearrange chicken pieces, placing large pieces at the outside of the dish. Cook 6 minutes longer or until fork-tender. Sprinkle with lemon pepper.

Yield: 4 servings.

Chicken Parmesan

4 to 6 boneless, skinless chicken breasts
⅓ cup melted margarine
1 cup grated parmesan cheese

Roll chicken in melted margarine first and then in parmesan cheese until well coated. Place chicken in a greased baking pan and drizzle a little extra margarine over each piece. Bake at 350° for 1 hour or until tender.

Pepperoni Chicken

6 boneless, skinless chicken breasts
24 pepperoni slices
6 mozzarella cheese slices

Brown chicken on both sides in a well greased skillet. Place chicken in a sprayed 9 x 13-inch pan. Arrange 4 pepperoni slices over each piece of chicken and bake at 350° for 20 minutes. Remove from oven, top each with cheese and bake 5 minutes or until chicken is tender.

Party Chicken

1 (2.25 ounce) package dried beef, sliced
4 boneless, skinless chicken breasts
2 (10½ ounce) cans cream of mushroom soup

Spread dried beef slices in bottom of a greased baking dish. Lay chicken over beef. Pour mushroom soup over chicken. Refrigerate 3 hours. Bake at 275° for 2½ hours or until chicken is tender.

Note: Sometimes I chop the dried beef, mix it with the soup and pour it over the chicken before baking. Sometimes I do not refrigerate this before baking. It's great either way. I serve this with wild rice, a cranberry-cherry gelatin salad and green beans.

Irma Mouttet's Sunday Chicken

4 boneless, skinless chicken breasts
1 (10½ ounce) can cream of mushroom soup
1½ cups shredded cheddar cheese

Place chicken in a greased 9 x 13-inch and pan bake at 350° for 30 minutes. Remove from oven and spread soup over chicken. Top with cheese. Bake 30 minutes longer.

Jim Wornall's Apple Jack Chicken

6 boneless, skinless chicken breasts
3 Jonathan apples, sliced thin
6 slices monterey jack cheese

Place chicken in a greased 9 x 13-inch pan. Bake at 350° for 40 minutes. Turn chicken over. Lay apple slices over each breast and bake 10 minutes. Remove from oven and top each piece with a slice of cheese. Bake 10 minutes longer or until cheese melts and chicken is tender.

Apricot Chicken

6 boneless, skinless chicken breasts
1 cup apricot nectar
1 (1 ounce) envelope dry onion soup mix

Arrange chicken breasts in a 9 x 13-inch pan. Pour apricot nectar over top. Sprinkle with soup mix. Cover with foil and bake at 350° for 1 hour. Remove cover and bake 15 minutes longer.

Chicken Lemonade

6 boneless, skinless chicken breasts
1 cup lemon juice
⅓ cup margarine, melted

Place chicken in a 9 x 13-inch glass dish. Cover with lemon juice and marinate for 1 hour in refrigerator, turning often. Drain juice off chicken and pour margarine over chicken. Bake at 350° for about 1 hour or until tender.

Yield: 6 servings.

Orange Soda-Pop Chicken

4 boneless, skinless chicken breasts
1 (12 ounce) can orange soda pop
2 tablespoons worcestershire sauce

Arrange chicken breasts in a microwave dish. Pour orange soda pop over chicken. Sprinkle with worcesterhire sauce. Cover with plastic wrap, folding back corner to vent. Microwave on high for 4 minutes. Rotate dish ½ turn, then cook 4 minutes. Rotate dish ½ turn. Chicken should be cooked until juice is clear and meat is not pink in center.

Yield: 4 servings.

Judy's Orange-Onion Chicken

4 boneless, skinless chicken breasts
1 cup orange juice
1 (1 ounce) envelope dry onion soup mix

Trim off any visible fat on the chicken. Spray a 9 x 13-inch pan with non-stick cooking spray, then arrange chicken pieces in the pan. Pour orange juice over chicken, then sprinkle with onion soup mix. Bake at 350° for 30 minutes. Turn chicken, then bake 30 minutes longer or until tender.

Chicken Jalapeno

4 boneless, skinless chicken breasts
2 tablespoons melted margarine
½ cup jalapeno jelly

Place chicken breasts between 2 sheets of heavy duty plastic wrap and flatten to ¼-inch thickness, using a meat mallet. Cook chicken in margarine in a large skillet over medium heat for 5 minutes on each side. Remove to a serving platter. Stir jelly into pan drippings and bring to a boil, stirring until smooth. Spoon over chicken.

Baked Breaded Chicken

4 boneless, skinless chicken breasts
½ cup mayonnaise
1¼ cups Italian seasoned breadcrumbs

Brush both sides of chicken with mayonnaise. Roll in crumbs until coated. Place in baking pan. Bake at 375° for 45 minutes or until there is no pink in chicken and juice runs clear when pierced with a fork.

Cornmeal Breaded Chicken

4 skinless, boneless chicken breasts
4 tablespoons milk
8 tablespoons cornmeal or enough to coat chicken

Rinse and dry chicken with paper towels. Dip each piece in milk. Roll in cornmeal until coated. Bake in a sprayed pan at 350° for 30 minutes. Turn and bake 20 to 30 minutes longer or until browned and fork tender.

Ritzy Baked Chicken

4 boneless, skinless chicken breasts
1 cup sour cream
1 cup crushed Cheezits crackers

Roll chicken breasts in sour cream, then in crushed crackers. Bake at 325° for 1 hour and 10 minutes or until tender.

Coca-Cola Barbequed Chicken

4 to 6 boneless, skinless chicken breasts
½ cup ketchup
1 (12 ounce) can Coca-Cola

Place chicken in large greased skillet. Combine ketchup and Coca-Cola; pour over chicken and cover. Cook at 350° for about 1 hour or until tender.

Barbequed Chicken

4 boneless, skinless chicken breasts
1 (12 ounce) can 7-Up
1 (8 ounce) bottle barbeque sauce

Place chicken in greased skillet. Combine 7-Up and barbecue sauce; pour over chicken. Bring to a boil then simmer for 1 hour or until tender.

Grilled Catalina Chicken

4 boneless, skinless chicken breast halves
½ cup Catalina dressing
¼ teaspoon black pepper

Trim all visible fat from chicken. Mix Catalina dressing and black pepper together. Pour into an oblong dish. Add chicken and turn to coat. Marinate chicken 4 to 6 hours or overnight. When ready to grill, prepare coals and grill chicken for 20 minutes over hot grill. Place marinade in saucepan and bring to a boil. Brush chicken with reserved, heated marinade.

Broiled Chicken Cordon Bleu

4 boneless, skinless chicken breasts
4 slices cheddar or Swiss cheese, divided
4 slices ham or Canadian bacon, fully cooked

Preheat broiler. Broil chicken breasts 4 inches from heat for 4 minutes. Turn chicken over and broil for 4 or 5 minutes or until tender. Cut cheese in half. Place ½ slice cheese on top of each chicken breast, then top the cheese with ham or Canadian bacon slice. Broil for about 30 seconds, then top with remaining ½ cheese slices. Broil until cheese melts.

Roast Chicken

1 (2½ pound) whole chicken
1 onion, peeled
5 tablespoons margarine, melted

Rinse chicken inside and out with cool water. Dry with paper towels. Place a peeled onion inside chicken cavity. Brush margarine over chicken. Tie legs together. Place in a foil-lined, broiler pan and roast chicken at 350° for 20 minutes per pound. Baste often with additional margarine. Chicken is done when it is pricked with a fork and the juice is clear.

Lois Davis' Orange Chicken

1 (2½ pound) chicken, cut in serving pieces
1 (12 ounce) can orange soda
¼ cup soy sauce

Place chicken pieces in a foil-lined, 9 x 13-inch pan that has been sprayed with non-stick spray. Mix together the orange soda and soy sauce, then pour it over the chicken. Bake at 350° for 1 hour or until chicken is tender. Baste chicken occasionally as it bakes.

Optional: If you don't want to cut up a chicken, buy the pieces you want. It's a lot easier.

Willie Copeland's
Southern Fried Chicken

1 (2 to 2½ pound) fryer chicken, cut in serving pieces
2 cups flour
1½ inches oil

Put flour (and desired seasonings) in a brown paper bag and shake 2 or 3 pieces of chicken at a time until well coated. Remove chicken from bag and shake off excess flour. Heat oil in a deep skillet. Place chicken, skin side down, in hot oil. Cook covered for 5 minutes. Remove cover and fry until bottom side is browned. Turn chicken once and fry on other side. Drain on paper towels.

Optional: If you don't want to cut up a chicken, buy your favorite pieces.

Baked Buttermilk Chicken

1 chicken, cut in serving pieces
½ cup buttermilk
1 cup Italian style breadcrumbs

Dip chicken in buttermilk, then roll it in breadcrumbs. Place on a sprayed, nonstick baking pan. Bake at 350° for about 1 hour or until tender.

Optional: If you don't want to cut up a chicken, buy your favorite pieces.

Chipper Chicken

1 (3 pound) chicken, cut in serving pieces
1 stick margarine, melted
3 cups potato chips, crushed

Dip chicken in melted margarine, then roll in crushed potato chips. Bake in a greased 9 x 13-inch pan at 350° for 1 hour or until tender.

Optional: If you don't want to cut up a chicken, buy your favorite
pieces.

Irish Chicken

1 (2½ pound) chicken, cut into serving pieces
1 egg, beaten
1½ cups dry potato flakes

Dip each chicken piece in egg, then roll in potato flakes. Repeat with all chicken pieces. Melt 1 stick margarine in a shallow baking pan, then place chicken in the pan and bake at 375° for 30 minutes. Turn chicken over and bake for 20 minutes more.

Optional: If you don't want to cut up a chicken, buy your favorite
pieces.

Oven-Fried Chicken

1 (2 to 3 pound) chicken, cut in serving pieces
¼ cup melted margarine
1 cup seasoned breadcrumbs

Wash and dry chicken. Coat each piece of chicken with melted margarine. Roll each piece in breadcrumbs coating well. Bake in a greased, 9 x 13-inch pan at 350° for 50 minutes to 1 hour.

Optional:　If you don't want to cut up a chicken, buy your favorite pieces.

Lois Rohm's Crisp Chicken

4 chicken breasts, halved, skinned, boned
2 eggs, beaten
Crushed corn flakes

Dip chicken in eggs, then roll in crushed corn flakes until wellcoated. Spray a baking sheet with cooking spray, place chicken on it and bake at 350° for about 1 hour.

Yield: 4 servings.

Chicken A La King

1 (10½ ounce) can cream of mushroom soup
2 (6 ounce) cans chicken, drained, chopped
1 package patty shells or toast points

Combine chicken and soup. Heat thoroughly. Prepare patty shells according to package directions or toast bread. To serve, pour hot chicken in patty shells or over toast points.

Optional:　To make toast points, make 2 diagonal cuts from corner to corner on bread slices. The resulting 4 triangles are the toast points.

152

Betty's Quesadillas

1 small onion, chopped
1 to 1½ cups shredded cheddar cheese
10 flour tortillas

Place desired amount of onion and cheese in center of a flour tortilla. Fold over and secure with wooden picks. Fry in melted margarine on both sides until golden brown.

Optional: You may add cooked, shredded chicken breast on top of the cheese and onion to make Chicken Quesadillas.

Dorothy Townsend's Apricot Cornish Hens

3 (1 pound) cornish hens, skinned
⅔ cup apricot nectar
3 tablespoons apricot jam, melted

Remove giblets from hens. Rinse hens under cold water and pat dry. Split each hen in half lengthwise, using an electric knife. Place hens in a 9 x 13-inch baking dish. Pour apricot nectar over them, turning to coat. Cover hens with foil and marinate in the refrigerator for 2 hours, turning occasionally. Remove hens from marinade, but reserve marinade. Bake uncovered in a 9 x 13-inch baking dish that is sprayed with a nonstick cooking spray at 350° for 20 minutes. Baste with marinade. Bake 20 minutes longer and baste with melted apricot jam. Bake 20 minutes more or until tender.

Yield: 6 servings.

Merle's Cornish Hen A La Orange

4 (18 ounce) cornish hens, rinsed, dried
3 tablespoons margarine, melted
1 (10 ounce) jar orange marmalade

Place hens in a greased, 9 x 13-inch baking pan. Mix together the melted margarine and orange marmalade; set aside. Bake hens at 350° for 30 minutes. Pour orange mixture over them and bake for 1 hour longer, basting several times.

Orange-Stuffed Roast Turkey

1 (12 pound) turkey, skinned
4 oranges, quartered
½ cup liquid butter buds
or non-fat, butter-flavored, cooking spray

Wash and dry turkey. Remove giblets and neck. Prepare butter buds according to package directions to make ½ cup of liquid butter buds. Rub on outside of turkey (or spray generously with a butter-flavored non-fat cooking spray). Fill cavity with orange quarters. Place turkey, breast up, on a rack in a roasting pan. Follow directions on turkey wrapping for roasting or roast at 325° for 3½ to 4 hours or until turkey is tender and juices run clear. Turkey should not be pink.

Serves about 20.

Roast Turkey

1 (12 to 16 pound) turkey
Melted margarine
Salt

Rinse turkey and pat dry with paper towels after removing giblets and neck. Place turkey, breast side up, on rack in roasting pan. Baste occasionally with melted margarine. Place a tent of foil over the turkey. Roast at 325° for 3½ to 5 hours for 12 to 16 pound turkey. Remove foil during the last ½ hour to brown. Turkey is done when you can "shake its leg" and juices run clear (no pink). Sprinkle with salt.

Foil-Wrapped Roast Turkey

1 (10 to 12 pound) frozen turkey
Small rolls, sliced
Mayonnaise

Thaw frozen turkey in original wrapping in refrigerator. After thawed, unwrap and wash turkey. Place turkey, breast up, in center of heavy foil. Bring one end of foil snugly over top of turkey, then bring the opposite end up, overlapping first. Fold foil down snugly at breast and legs. Place bird in bottom of roaster and roast turkey at 350º for 3 to 4 hours. About 15 minutes before turkey is done, remove from oven. Fold foil away from bird so it is not covered and roast until golden brown and tender. Let set for 20 minutes.

Cook 14 to 16-pound turkey for 4 to 5 hours. Cook 18 to 20-pound turkey for 5 to 6 hours. Cooking times may vary with ovens.

Mushroom-Onion Roast

1 (3 to 4 pound) chuck roast
1 (10¾ ounce) can cream of mushroom soup
½ package dry onion soup mix

Brown or sear meat on all sides. (This step can be omitted, but the roast tastes better if it is seared.) Place roast on 2 to 3 thicknesses of foil. Spread soup over meat, then sprinkle with onion soup mix. Wrap roast tightly. Place in pan and bake at 325° for 3 to 4 hours or until done.

Onion Roast

1 (3 pound) rump or chuck roast
1 (1 ounce) envelope dry onion soup
½ teaspoon garlic powder

Place a beef roast on a large sheet of foil. Sprinkle 1 package of onion soup mix over the meat. Sprinkle roast with dash garlic powder. Seal foil. Place in large pan and bake at 325° for 1½ hours or until tender (or bake at 200° for 8 to 9 hours, depending on the size of the roast).

Crock Pot Roast Beef

4 potatoes, peeled, quartered
2 onions, sliced, divided
1 (3 to 4 pound) roast

Place half of the potatoes and onions in the bottom of a crock pot. Lay beef roast on top of the vegetables, then add the remaining potatoes and onions on top of the meat. Pour ½ cup water over the meat and vegetables. Cover and cook on low for 10 to 12 hours or on high for 5 to 6 hours. Season to taste.

Electric Skillet Roast Beef

1 (3 pound) beef roast
1 large onion, chopped
1 teaspoon black pepper

Heat 3 tablespoons oil in electric skillet to 350°. Place roast in skillet and brown each side and sprinkle with black pepper. Top with onions. Reduce heat to 250°. Add water, filling skillet halfway up. Cover with lid and cook for about 3 hours or until fork tender.

Marjorie's Beef Roast

1 teaspoon seasoned salt
2 tablespoons brown sugar
1 (3 pound) beef roast

Rub salt and brown sugar on all sides of roast. Place beef in a roaster or heavy pan. Add ½ cup water to pan. Roast at 325° for about 3 hours or until tender.

Caraway Seed Roast

1 (3 pound) rump roast
1 tablespoon caraway seed
1 teaspoon garlic powder

Trim all visible fat from meat. Sprinkle caraway seeds and garlic powder over rump roast. Place on rack in roaster and cover or wrap in foil and bake dry at 325° for 3 hours or until tender. The caraway seeds give a good flavor. The drippings make a delicious gravy.

Mother's Pot Roast With Vegetables

1 (3 to 4 pound) beef roast
6 carrots, scraped, cut into 3 pieces
4 potatoes, peeled

Spray or pour a little oil in a heavy skillet or dutch oven. Lay roast on it and sear or brown meat on medium high heat on all sides. Pour 2 inches of water around the meat; cover and heat on low for 2½ to 3 hours or until tender. Add quartered potatoes and carrots to the pot about 1 hour before roast is done. Season to taste.

Rosebillie Horn's
Old-Fashioned Roast Beef

3 pound beef roast
½ cup flour
1 to 2 sliced onions

Dredge beef in flour. Place in greased skillet and brown on all sides to seal in juices. Lay sliced onions on top of roast. Pour ½ cup water over all. Cover and bake at 325° for 2½ hours. Remove cover and bake for 30 minutes longer.

Optional: After baking for 2 hours, you may add potatoes and carrots, then bake for 1 hour longer.

Pat Meyers' Dill Pickle Roast

1 (3 pound) eye of round beef roast
Juice from 1 pint jar dill pickles
1 cup dill pickles

Place roast in a pan which has a lid. Pour juice over roast.
Cover with lid or foil and bake at 325° for about 3 hours or
until tender and done to your taste. Serve pickles in a side
dish with roast.

Yield: 12 servings.

Yankee Pot Roast

1 (4 to 5 pound) beef pot roast
2 (10½ ounce) cans French onion soup
6 potatoes, peeled, quartered

Brown meat on all sides in a greased iron skillet or dutch
oven. Add soup. Cover and cook on low heat on top of
stove for 3 to 4 hours or until roast is fork tender. Add
potatoes after meat has cooked for 2 hours and continue
cooking until done.

Cracked Pepper Roast

1 (3 pound) beef eye of round roast
⅓ cup black peppercorns, crushed
Salt

Trim fat from roast. Press pepper over entire surface of
meat. Place roast on rack of broiler pan sprayed with
cooking spray. Cover with foil and bake at 450° for 20
minutes. Reduce heat to 300º uncover and bake 2-3 hours
longer or until the meat thermometer reads 160° for medium
or 170° for well done in the thickest part of the roast.
Sprinkle with salt. Let stand 15 minutes before slicing
diagonally across grain into thin slices.

159

Buttermilk Baked Roast

1 (3 to 4 pound) beef roast
½ cup buttermilk
1 (1 ounce) envelope dry onion soup mix

Trim off all visible fat. Place foil on a cookie sheet and place roast on top. Drizzle buttermilk over meat and sprinkle onion soup mix over roast. Wrap up foil and bake at 275° for 5 hours or to desired doneness. Drain well.

Baked Pot Roast and Peppers

1 (3 to 4 pound) beef pot roast
1 (10½ ounce) can beef consomme
1 green and 1 red bell pepper, sliced or chopped

Brown roast on all sides in a greased skillet. Place in a roasting pan and pour consomme and 1 cup water evenly over beef. Cover tightly and bake at 325° for 1 hour. Reduce heat to 275° and bake 4 hours longer or until done. Add bell peppers 20 minutes before roast is finished cooking.
Optional: Serve with 2 preparedpackages of beef-flavored Ramen noodles.

Coffee Beef Roast

1 (3-5 pound) beef roast
1 cup vinegar
2 cups black coffee

Place roast in a glass dish or pan. Pour vinegar over meat. Cover and refrigerate for 24 hours or longer; drain. Place roast in a large skillet and brown on all sides. Pour 2 cups strong black coffee over the meat. Add 2 cups water and cover. Simmer on top of stove for 4 to 6 hours (depending on the size or roast). Add more water if needed.

Yield: 6 to 10 servings.

Overnight Brisket

2 tablespoons liquid smoke
1 (3 to 4 pound) beef brisket
Garlic powder

Rub 2 tablespoons liquid smoke on the sides of brisket.
Sprinkle with garlic powder. Wrap tightly in foil. Refrigerate
overnight. The next day sprinkle with more garlic powder.
Rewrap in foil. Bake in 9 x 13-inch dish (or whatever size is
needed) at 275° for 6 hours or at 325° for 5 hours.
Refrigerate overnight again. Next day, slice. If desired, pour
barbecue sauce over it and reheat.

Good Night Beef Brisket

1 (6 pound) brisket, trimmed
Worcestershire sauce
Seasoned salt

Place brisket, lean side up, in a baking pan about the same
size as brisket. Sprinkle worcestershire sauce generously
over meat. Smooth on meat with the back of a spoon.
Sprinkle seasoned salt over brisket. Turn brisket over, fat
side up, and repeat seasoning process. Cover tightly and
refrigerate overnight. Remove from refrigerator 30 minutes
before cooking, then roast at 300°, uncovered, for about 4
hours or until fork tender. Baste only with liquid that forms in
bottom of pan. Don't add water. Slice across grain.

Boiled Brisket

1 (3 to 4 pound) beef brisket
1 onion, quartered
3 celery ribs and tops, cut in 2-inch pieces

Place brisket in a pot with enough water to almost cover the meat. Add 1 quartered onion and celery tops and pieces. Cover with tight lid and simmer for 3 to 4 hours or until the meat is tender. Serve with horseradish sauce.

Marilyn Weaver's Sauce For Brisket

1 (8 ounce) bottle chili sauce
1 (12 ounce) can Coca-Cola, not diet
1 (1 ounce) envelope dry onion soup mix

Combine the 3 ingredients and mix well. Makes 2½ cups of sauce.

To prepare brisket, place a 3 to 4 pound brisket in roaster with a lid. Pour sauce over it. Cover and bake at 325° for 3 to 5 hours or for 30 minutes per pound until tender. Pour off sauce and serve in a gravy bowl with brisket.

Texas Brisket

1 (6 pound) boneless beef brisket
2 tablespoons worcestershire sauce
4 tablespoons bottle liquid smoke

Place brisket in a pan, and pour sauce and liquid smoke over brisket. Cover and bake at 275° for 5 to 7 hours or until tender.

Barbecued Beef Brisket

1 (4 pound) brisket
1 (3½ ounce) bottle liquid smoke
1 (6 to 8 ounce) bottle barbecue sauce

Place brisket in a baking pan. Pour liquid smoke over meat and rub into brisket. Cover and refrigerate overnight. Next day, bake covered at 275° for 5 hours. Remove from oven. Slice. Pour barbecue sauce over brisket, then reheat before serving.

Nancy McDonald's Soy Brisket

1 (3 to 4 pound) beef brisket
½ cup soy sauce
Dash garlic powder

Poke holes in brisket. Rub soy sauce in until brisket turns brown. Sprinkle with garlic powder. Bake covered with foil at 250° for 6 to 8 hours, or until tender.

Party Brisket

1 (5 pound) beef brisket
1 (6 ounce) can frozen lemon juice concentrate
1 (1 ounce) envelope dry onion soup mix

Trim off all visible fat from brisket. Stir enough thawed, lemon juice concentrate into the onion soup mix to make a smooth paste. Place brisket in a 9 x 13-inch pan or in a roasting pan. Spread lemon-onion paste over meat. Cover tightly with foil or a lid. Bake at 250° for 5 to 6 hours or until fork tender.

Yield: 10 to 12 servings.

Optional: Stir a little worcestershire sauce into lemon onion paste; spread on brisket, then bake.

163

Husband's Favorite Flank Steak

1 (2 pound) beef flank steak
⅓ cup soy sauce
⅓ cup worcestershire sauce

Score flank steak with a sharp knife and place in a glass dish. Combine soy sauce and worcestershire sauce and pour marinade over steak. Marinate steak in the refrigerator for 2 to 4 hours. Turn steak several times. Remove steak from marinade and broil or grill steak to desired doneness. Turn with tongs and broil other side. Let set 10 minutes before slicing. Slice across the grain, diagonally, into thin strips.

Steak Dinner Pockets

4 sirloin tip steaks
2 onions, sliced
4 potatoes, sliced

Place meat on foil and top with layers of sliced onions and potatoes. Seal foil into packages and place in pan. Bake at 350° for 1 hour.

Velma Stewart's Celery Steak

1 pound round steak
1 (10½ ounce) can cream of celery soup
½ teaspoon garlic salt

Place steak in a greased 9 x 13-inch pan. Spread soup over it. Sprinkle with garlic salt; cover with foil. Bake at 350° for 1 hour or until tender. Baste once or twice with soup during cooking.

164

South Seas Flank Steak

¼ cup soy sauce
¼ cup pineapple juice
1 flank steak

Pour soy sauce and pineapple juice in a shallow 9 x 13-inch dish. Lay flank steak in mixture and turn to coat both sides. Marinate one hour, turning every 15 minutes. Remove steak from marinade and broil or grill.

Mushroom Steak

1 (1 pound) round steak
1 (10½ ounce) can cream of mushroom soup
1 (4 ounce) can sliced mushrooms, drained

Place a round steak in a 9 x 13-inch pan lined with foil. Pour 1 can mushroom soup over steak and top with mushrooms. Cover with foil. Bake at 350° for 1 hour.

Swiss Steak

2 pounds round steak
1 sliced onion
1 (15 ounce) can tomato sauce with onions and peppers

Trim fat and pound steak thin. Place in a greased 9 x 13-inch pan. Top with onion slices, then pour tomato sauce over it. Cover and bake at 350° for 1½ hours. Uncover and bake for 15 minutes longer. Baste occasionally with tomato sauce. Bake until tender.

Optional: You may lay slices of Swiss cheese over each serving as soon as it is taken out of the oven.

Baked Cube Steaks

4-6 (8 ounce) cube steaks
2 cups water
Flour

Flour cube steaks and brown in greased skillet. Add 2 cups water and bake covered at 350° about 2 hours or until tender.

Yield: 4 to 6 servings.

Onita Copeland's Chicken Fried Steak

1 pound minute steaks or sirloin steak, cut in serving pieces
1 cup flour
1 to 2 beaten eggs

Trim fat and pound steak thin. Roll steaks in flour and dip in well beaten eggs, then roll in flour again. Fry on both sides in hot oil until browned.

Broiled T-Bone Steaks

4 T-bone steaks
½ teaspoon black pepper
1 teaspoon garlic powder or seasoned salt

Make a few diagonal cuts in the fat around the steak so it won't curl when broiling. Place the steaks on the broiler pan, which has been lined with foil. Broil 5 minutes on one side. Turn and broil 5 minutes on the other side. Continue cooking to desired doneness if steaks are too rare. Sprinkle with pepper and garlic powder.

Mock Fillet Mignon

2 pounds ground round steak
1 (1 ounce) envelope dry onion soup mix
6 bacon slices

Combine ground round and onion soup mix. Shape into 6 thick patties. Wrap a slice of bacon around each and secure with wooden picks. Place in a 9 x 13-inch dish and bake at 450° for 15 to 20 minutes or broil on each side.

Homemade Chorizo Sausage

1 onion, chopped
1 pound ground sirloin
1 package chili seasoning mix

Combine all ingredients and mix well. Cover and refrigerate overnight to blend flavors. Use in recipes requiring spicy meat, soups, casseroles and Mexican dishes such as burritos and tacos.

Mock Hungarian Goulash

1 pound ground beef or ground round
½ (10 ounce) package shell macaroni
1 (16 ounce) jar spaghetti sauce with chunky tomatoes and onions

Brown meat and drain. Prepare macaroni according to package directions. Combine the beef, macaroni and spaghetti sauce; mix the ingredients together and heat 10 minutes. Serve hot.

167

Hamburger-Potato Casserole

2 pounds ground beef
1 (10½ ounce) can cream of mushroom soup
1 (1 pound) package tater tots

Form ingredients into 3 layers. As the bottom layer, press hamburger into a greased, 9 x 13-inch pan. Spread soup over the meat. The tater tots form the third and top layer. Bake the casserole at 350° for 45 to 55 minutes.

Optional: Potatoes could be second layer, then top with soup.

Cory Rigg's Barbecue Beef

1 pound ground sirloin or ground beef
½ cup packed brown sugar
16 ounces barbeque sauce

Brown, crumble and drain meat. Stir in brown sugar and barbecue sauce. Cover and simmer for 15 minutes, stirring often. Spoon onto heated, hamburger buns

Chili

2 pounds ground beef or ground round
2 (1.25 ounce) envelopes chili seasoning
2 (32 ounce) jars spaghetti sauce with chunky tomatoes,
onions and peppers

Brown meat in a heavy skillet; drain. Stir in chili seasoning. Add sauce and 1 cup water; mix well. Simmer for 30 minutes.

Optional: You may add 1 or 2 cans pinto beans and heat for 20 minutes longer.

Juanita's Stuffed Green Peppers

1 pound ground beef or ground round, browned, drained
1 (15 ounce) can Spanish rice
4 green peppers, seeded

Blanch green peppers into boiling water and cook for several minutes. Remove and dip into cold water to stop the cooking process. This brings out the flavor and color of the peppers. Cool. Cut off tops of peppers; remove seeds and membranes. Stuff with mixture of cooked hamburger and Spanish rice. Bake at 350° for 20 minutes.

Optional: You may stuff peppers that have not been boiled or blanched. Place them in a greased casserole and bake at 350° for 25 minutes. Add a little water to the dish before baking the peppers.

Speedy Spaghetti

1 (16 ounce) package spaghetti
1 pound ground beef
1 (1 pound 10 ounce) jar chunky garden-style spaghetti sauce with extra tomatoes, garlic and onions

Prepare spaghetti according to package directions. Brown meat; crumble and drain. Stir spaghetti sauce into the meat and heat thoroughly. Pour drained spaghetti onto a large platter and spread meat sauce over spaghetti or combine spaghetti and meat sauce and mix thoroughly.

Creamed Beef Over Rice

1 pound ground beef
1 (10½ ounce) can golden cream of mushroom soup
2 cups cooked rice

Brown beef in a skillet, crumble and drain. Stir in soup, diluted with ½ can water or milk. Stir and simmer for 20 minutes. Serve over hot rice.

Spanish Meatloaf

1 pound ground beef
1 (16 ounce) can Spanish rice, drained
1 egg, beaten

Combine all ingredients and mix well. Pour into a greased loaf pan. Bake at 350° for 1 hour. Drain off excess liquid.

Optional: You may add 1 small chopped onion before baking.

Onion Burgers

2 pounds ground beef
1 (1 ounce) envelope dry onion soup mix
½ cup water

Combine hamburger with onion soup mix and water, mixing well. Shape into 8 burgers. Place burgers in a baking dish and cook uncovered at 350° for 15 minutes or until browned. Serve on hamburger buns.

Oriental Burgers

1½ pounds ground sirloin or ground round
½ cup chopped water chestnuts
½ cup teriyaki sauce

Combine meat and water chestnuts. Shape into 6 burgers and place in glass baking dish. Pour teriyaki sauce over burgers. Marinate covered in refrigerator for several hours or overnight. When ready to cook, fry in a skillet until brown on both sides. Serve as a main dish or as a sandwich.

Hamburger Steak With Mushrooms

1½ pounds hamburger or ground round steak
3 to 4 tablespoons margarine
½ pound mushrooms, cleaned, sliced

Shape hamburger or ground round steak into 4 large patties. Fry on both sides to desired doneness. In a separate skillet, melt margarine. Saute mushrooms in melted margarine, stirring often, for about 5 minutes. Drain. Place a hamburger steak on each dinner plate. Top with sauteed mushrooms.

Hamburger Stroganoff

1 pound ground beef or ground round
2 (10¾ ounce) cans cream of mushroom soup
1 (16 ounce) package noodles

Brown hamburger; drain. Stir soups into the crumbled hamburger and mix well. Cook for 10 minutes or until thoroughly heated; stir often. Boil noodles according to package directions; drain. Serve hamburger mixture over noodles.

Optional: You may brown a chopped onion with ground beef.

Kids' Favorite Casserole

1 pound ground beef
2 tablespoons chopped onion
1 (15 ounce) can baked beans

Brown ground beef and onion together; drain well. Stir in baked beans and cook until thoroughly heated.

Hobo Dinner

1 pound ground beef
4 onion slices
4 potatoes

Shape ground beef into patties. Slice potatoes ½-inch thick. Place patties on square of foil. Top with potato slices (2 to 3), then a slice of onion. Season to taste. Fold tightly; place in pan and bake at 350° for 45 minutes.

Optional: You may season hamburger with 1 teaspoon seasoned salt.

Chili Pie

4 cups corn chips, divided
2 (15 ounce) cans chili
1⅓ cups shredded cheddar cheese

Place 1 cup corn chips on 4 plates. Top with 1 cup hot chili on each. Sprinkle ⅓ cup cheese over chili and serve.

Optional: You may sprinkle chopped onions over cheese.

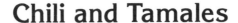

Chili and Tamales

1 (15 ounce) can tamales
1 (15 ounce) can chili without beans
½ cup shredded cheddar cheese

Heat tamales and remove papers. Heat chili. Place 2 tamales on each serving plate. Pour hot chili over tamales and top with cheese.

Optional: You may sprinkle chopped onion over cheese.

Chili Casserole

2 (15 ounce) cans chili con carne
2 to 3 cups corn chips
1 cup shredded cheddar cheese

Place alternate layers of chili and corn chips in a greased, casserole dish. Top with cheese. Cover. Bake at 350° for 30 minutes.

Optional: You may add 1 chopped onion over the chili.

Beef Tips and Noodles

1½ pounds stew meat, fat trimmed
2 (10½ ounce) cans cream of onion soup, diluted
1 (8 ounce) package noodles

Brown stew meat in a greased skillet. When browned, add soup diluted with 1 cup water. Allow to simmer for 3 hours, stirring occasionally. Cook noodles according to package directions. Serve beef tips over noodles.

Shredded Beef For Tacos

2 pounds lean beef round steak
1 tablespoon minced garlic
1 cup water

Rinse meat and trim off fat. Cut into 4 pieces. Place meat, garlic and water in a crockpot. Cook on high for 2 hours. Reduce heat and cook on low for 6 or 7 hours or until tender. Remove meat and broth to a bowl. Refrigerate 2 hours. Skim off fat. Remove meat and shred into bite-sized pieces.

No-Peek Stew

2 pounds beef stew meat, fat trimmed
1 (10½ ounce) can cream of mushroom soup
1 package dry onion soup mix

In a Dutch oven or roaster combine all ingredients and mix well. Stir in 1 cup water. Cover and bake at 325° for 2½ hours. Do not peek! Serve over rice or noodles.

Ann's Beef Fondue

4 (8 ounce) fillets mignon, cut into 1-inch cubes
2 cups vegetable oil
Sauce of your choice

Prepare ½ pound fillet per person. Heat 2 cups oil on stove until hot. Watch carefully. Pour oil into fondue pot. Place pot above burner on table. Give each person his own fondue fork. Spear meat on fork and cook in oil in fondue pot to desired doneness. Remove meat to plate and dip in choice of sauces offered such as mustard sauce, sour cream and onion sauce, chili sauce, B.B.Q. sauce, etc.

Yield: 4 servings.

Beef Kabobs

2 pounds sirloin tips, cut into bite-size pieces
Green peppers, cubed
Cherry tomatoes

Alternate beef, peppers and cherry tomatoes on long skewers. Place on a grill 4 to 5 inches above hot coals. Turn occasionally. Cook until meat is brown to desired doneness.

Optional: You may brush beef and vegetables with melted margarine or barbecue sauce.

John Beuscher's Incredible Ribs

1 slab beef ribs
1 tablespoon seasoning salt
1 (8 ounce) bottle Italian dressing

Spread coals evenly in grill. Open bottom vent ½ way and light coals. Place ribs, bone down, in bottom layer of foil. "Paint" ribs with dressing. Sprinkle with seasoning. Cover top with foil. When fire is out on coals, place wrapped ribs on grill and cover. Close top vent till only a light is visible. Cook for 6 hours, turning ribs every 2 hours. At hour 6, remove foil top and puncture bottom foil to drain.

Optional: You may coat with barbecue sauce and cook 45 to 60 minutes more.

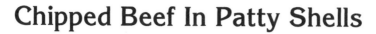

Chipped Beef In Patty Shells

6 frozen patty shells
1 (11 ounce) package frozen creamed chipped beef
6 parsley sprigs

Bake patty shells according to package directions. Prepare chipped beef according to package directions. To serve, place a patty shell in each serving plate and fill with chipped beef. Top with a sprig of parsley.

Optional: You may add 1 (8 ounce) can drained peas or corn to the chipped beef.

Margie Luben's Corned Beef Brisket

1 (3 to 4 pound) corned beef brisket
2 tablespoons prepared mustard
4 tablespoons brown sugar

Cook corned beef in a pot of water on top of the stove over low heat for 2½ hours. Remove from pot. Place beef in a 9 x 13-inch pan or a roaster or broiler pan, then poke holes in the meat with fork. Mix mustard and brown sugar together until creamy and a paste is formed. Spread mixture over entire brisket. Bake at 350° for 1½ hours or until tender.

Creamed Dried Beef

2 (2.25 ounces) packages thinly sliced, dried beef, chopped
3 tablespoons flour
2½ cups hot milk

Fry thin dried beef slices in a well greased skillet until crisp. Stir in flour with beef, slowly add milk and cook until thickened, stirring constantly. (The beef is so salty that no salt should be added.) Serve hot over crisp toast.

Corned Beef and Cabbage

1 (4 to 6 pound) corned beef, boneless brisket
1 head cabbage, cored, quartered
6 potatoes

Cover beef with cold water and bring to a boil. Lower heat and simmer for 4 hours or until tender. Drain off most of the water. Add potatoes and cook for 20 minutes. Add cabbage and cook for about 12 minutes longer or until all 3 ingredients are fork tender.

Optional: You may add onion, cut in quarters.

New England Corned Beef

1 (4 pound) corned beef brisket
20 whole cloves
½ cup pure maple syrup

Place beef in a large roaster, cover with water and bring to a boil. Reduce heat, cover with a lid and simmer until done for 3½ to 4 hours. Remove from water and place on a rack in a roasting pan. Score the top and stud with cloves. Pour pure maple syrup over meat and bake at 375° for about 15 minutes or until browned and glazed. Baste during cooking.

Roast Leg of Lamb

1 (6 pound) leg of lamb
⅓ cup honey
6 tablespoons soy sauce, divided

Trim fat off lamb and place on a rack in a shallow pan.
Brush with honey. Pour water in pan to depth of ¾-inch.
Bake lamb at 450° for 30 minutes. Reduce heat to 350°.
Pour half of soy sauce over lamb and roast for 3 to 3½ hours
longer or 35 minutes per pound. Baste lamb every 30
minutes with remaining soy sauce and pan drippings.

Leg of Lamb

1 (6 pound) leg of lamb
2 cups water
2 cups cider vinegar

Place lamb on roaster rack. Mix water and vinegar together
and pour over lamb. Cover and cook at 400° for 3 hours (30
minutes per pound). Baste frequently. Remove cover to let
lamb brown and cook 15 minutes longer. Good with mint
sauce.

Charcoal-Broiled Lamb Chops

4 to 6 loin lamb chops
Olive oil
Lime Juice

Marinate chops in 4 parts olive oil to 1 part lime juice.
Charcoal broil to desired doneness.

178

Dijon Pork Chops

6 loin pork chops
½ cup packed brown sugar
2 teaspoons dijon mustard

Arrange pork chops in a greased baking dish. Combine sugar and mustard in a small dish, mixing well. Spread the mixture on top of chops. Bake covered at 350° for 45 minutes. Uncover and bake about 10 minutes longer or until browned.

Onion Pork Chops

6 pork chops
1 (10½ ounce) can condensed French onion soup
1 tablespoon prepared mustard

Arrange pork chops in a greased baking dish. In a bowl, combine the onion soup and mustard, mixing well. Pour over pork chops; cover and bake at 350° for 30 minutes. Uncover and bake another 15 to 20 minutes or until pork chops are browned. Serve over hot, cooked rice.

Barbecued Pork Chops

4 to 6 pork chops
1 cup ketchup
2 cups Coca-Cola, not diet

Brown pork chops in greased skillet. Combine Coke and ketchup; pour over chops. Cover with lid or foil and simmer about 1 hour or until tender.

Pork Chop Special

4 to 6 pork chops
½ cup rice, cooked
2 (10½ ounce) cans cream of mushroom soup

Brown pork chops on both sides; drain. Place cooked rice in bottom of a greased baking dish. Lay browned chops over rice. Pour soup over pork chops. Cover and bake at 375° for 40 minutes.

Cranberry-Glazed Pork Roast

1 (6 pound) pork shoulder roast
1 (16 ounce) can whole cranberry sauce
¼ cup packed brown sugar

Place pork on rack in a roaster pan and roast at 325° for 3 hours or until fork tender. (If using a meat thermometer, it should register 185°.) Remove roast and pour off drippings. Trim off skin and fat. Return meat to pan. Mash cranberry sauce with a fork, then stir in brown sugar and mix well. Cut deep gashes in meat and brush generously with cranberry sauce. Bake at 350° for about 30 minutes, brushing often with glaze.

Easy Pork Loin Roast

1 (1 ounce) envelope dry onion soup mix
1 (4 to 5 pound) pork loin roast
1 teaspoon dried rosemary

Place large piece of heavy-duty foil in a 9 x 13-inch baking pan. Sprinkle soup in the middle of the foil. Place roast on the top of the soup mix. Sprinkle with dried rosemary. Fold foil over and seal securely, folding up ends of foil. Bake at 300° for 3½ to 4 hours or until done to your preference.

Crown Roast Pork

1 (6 to 8 pound) pork loin with ribs
Parsley
Crab apples (enough for one on each bone end)

Ask your butcher to make the crown from 2 strips of pork loin containing about 20 ribs. Remove backbone. Season to taste. Place roast in roasting pan, bone ends up. Wrap bone ends in foil. Roast uncovered at 325° for 2 to 3 hours, or until well done and tender. To serve, replace foil wraps with crab apples or paper frills. Garnish platter with parsley.

Optional: After cooking, you may season pork loin by sprinkling meat with ½ teaspoon seasoned salt.

Roast Loin of Pork

1 (3 pound) boneless pork loin roast
1 teaspoon powdered mustard
1 teaspoon marjoram leaves

Place roast on a rack in a shallow baking pan. Combine dry mustard and marjoram leaves; rub over surface of roast. Insert a meat thermometer and roast at 350° for 30 to 35 minutes per pound or until the thermometer reads 170° and meat is done. Pork should be cooked thoroughly. Slice and serve.

Pennsylvania Dutch
Pork and Sauerkraut

2 tablespoons margarine
1 (2½ pound) tenderloin of pork
2 (15 ounce) cans sauerkraut

Melt margarine in a heavy iron skillet or dutch oven and brown the pork on both sides. Cover and cook tenderloin over low heat for 20 minutes. Add sauerkraut. Cover and continue to simmer for 1 hour or until tenderloin is thoroughly cooked. Serve with mashed potatoes and applesauce for an authentic Pennsylvania Dutch dinner.

Amish Pork Roast

1 (3 to 4 pound) pork roast
1 (27 ounce) can sauerkraut, drained
3 cups water

Place pork roast in center of roast pan. Arrange sauerkraut around meat. Pour water over roast. Cover and bake at 325° for 2½ to 3 hours. Add more water if sauerkraut dries during baking.

Southwestern Pork Tenderloin

1 pound pork tenderloin
3 tablespoons water
½ cup chunky salsa

Place tenderloin in a glass dish and add water. Cover with a layer of 2 paper towels. Microwave on high for 5 minutes. Turn pork over, cover with paper towels and cook on high for 5 minutes longer. Remove paper towels and drain. Pour sauce over meat and microwave uncovered for 5 to 8 minutes or until done on medium heat. Let stand 3 minutes before slicing.

Yield: 4 servings.

Herbed Pork Tenderloin

2 (¾ pound) pork tenderloins
2 tablespoons black pepper
2 tablespoons chopped fresh rosemary

Sprinkle tenderloins with pepper (freshly ground pepper is best) and with rosemary. Grill, covered with grill lid, at 350° for 15 to 18 minutes or until a meat thermometer inserted into thickest portions registers 170°, turning occasionally. Slice in thin slices to serve.

Ham Jubilee

1 fully cooked, smoked ham slice
¼ teaspoon ground cloves
1 (20 ounce) can cherry pie filling

Place ham slice in a greased 9 x 13-inch pan. Sprinkle with cloves. Cover and bake at 350º for 30 minutes or until heated. Cut into serving pieces. Pour cherry pie filling into a saucepan and heat, stirring often. Spoon over ham. Serve as an accompaniment.

Pepsi Ham

1 (10 to 12 pound) boneless ham, cooked
Whole cloves
2 cups Pepsi-Cola (not diet), divided

Score ham. Stud with whole cloves. Place ham in a roaster. Pour 1 cup Pepsi over ham. Cover tightly with lid or foil. Bake at 325° for 2 hours. Baste occasionally with the second cup of Pepsi during the last 30 minutes of cooking time.

Honey Ham

1 (5 pound) boneless, fully-cooked ham
¼ cup honey
½ cup packed brown sugar

Score ham. Wrap in foil and bake at 325° for 1 hour in a broiler pan. Combine honey and brown sugar, mixing well. Remove ham from oven. Pull foil open and spread honey glaze over ham. Rewrap in foil and bake for 1 hour longer. Cool for 15 minutes before serving.

Judy McDonald Hutchinson's Ham and Red-Eye Gravy

4 slices country ham
Strong black coffee
Hot sauce

Fry ham slices in heavy skillet, turning frequently. Remove ham slices. Add coffee to skillet (in the amount of gravy desired). Simmer, stir and scrape the pan. Add hot sauce to taste. Serve with ham.

Ham and Limas

1 (10 ounce) package frozen, baby lima beans
1 center-cut ham slice
½ cup grated cheddar cheese

Cook frozen beans until tender, according to package directions and drain. Place ham slice in a shallow pan and broil 5 minutes on each side, 3 inches from heat. Arrange beans over ham. Sprinkle with shredded cheese and broil only until cheese melts and bubbles.

Ham-Stuffed Tomatoes

1 pint cherry tomatoes
2 (2¼ ounce) cans deviled ham
2 tablespoon horseradish

About 3 hours before serving, slice tops from tomatoes. Scoop out pulp and mix with ham and horseradish. Fill tomatoes. Refrigerate about 3 hours.

Yield: About 20.

Hawaiian Ham Steaks

1 (8½ ounce) can sliced pineapple with juice
2 tablespoons brown sugar
1 (1 pound) center-cut ham steak

Pour ½-inch juice into a skillet. Stir in 2 tablespoons brown sugar. Make slashes in fat around steak to keep it from curling. Place ham in skillet with juice mixture. Top with pineapple slices. Cook on medium low heat. Turn twice. Cook until sauce becomes a thick syrup. Serve with pineapple slice on each serving.

Broiled Ham and Pineapple

1 (1½ pound) fully cooked ham slice
1 (8¼ ounce) can sliced pineapple
Butter or margarine, softened

Trim fat on ham. Diagonally cut edge of fat on ham at 1-inch intervals to prevent curling. Place ham on a rack in a broiler pan and broil 4 inches from heat for 5 minutes. Turn and broil 3 minutes on the other side. Place drained pineapple slices on ham and brush with butter. Broil 2 minutes longer or until ham is light brown.

Apricot-Glazed Ham

1 (29 ounce) can apricots, with syrup
¾ cup apricot preserves
1 (4 pound) baked, boneless ham

Drain syrup from apricots. Reserve fruit. Bring syrup to a boil; reduce heat and simmer until liquid is reduced to half, about 10 minutes. Remove from heat. Stir in preserves and apricots. Set aside. Bake ham at 325° for 2 hours. Baste ham often with glaze during the last hour of baking and serve remainder with ham.

Apple Cider Ham

1 (5 pound) cooked, boneless ham
12 whole cloves
2 cups apple cider, divided

Score ham and place whole cloves in it. Pour a cup of cider over the ham. Cover and bake at 325° for 2 hours. Baste occasionally with the second cup of cider.

Baked Canned Ham

1 canned ham
Whole cloves
Brown sugar

Score and stud ham with whole cloves over entire surface. Pat brown sugar thickly over surface. Wrap tightly in heavy-duty, aluminum foil and bake at 450° for 30 minutes. Open foil and baste ham with syrup that has formed. Pat more brown sugar on top. Reduce heat to 350°, open foil, and bake for 30 minutes longer. The crust of the ham should be sugary and crisp. Slice thinly. Serve on biscuits.

Ham and Noodles Romanoff

1 (7.75 ounce) box noodles Romanoff mix
1½ cup cooked, cubed ham
1 (8 ounce) can cut green beans, drained

Prepare noodles according to package directions, but increase milk to ⅔ cup. Stir in ham and green beans. Bake in a greased, covered 1½-quart casserole dish at 350° for 20 minutes.

Yield: 4 servings.

187

Crescent Pizza

1 (8 ounce) can crescent dinner rolls
1 (3½ ounce) package pepperoni slices
1 (8 ounce) package shredded mozzarella cheese

Separate crescent rolls into 4 rectangles and seal perforations. Arrange 8 pepperoni slices on each 5 x 7-inch rectangle. Top with cheese. Place on a greased baking sheet and bake at 375° for 14 to 16 minutes or until crust is golden brown.

Optional: Before placing pepperoni and cheese on pizza, you may spread a prepared pizza sauce on the crescent roll dough, then top it with pepperoni and cheese and bake.

Sauteed Apples

4 to 6 apples, peeled, cored, sliced
1 cup flour
3 tablespoons margarine, melted

Roll apples in flour, then saute in melted margarine until golden brown.   Serve with ham or roast pork.

Optional: You may sprinkle with sugar or cinnamon.

Ham Sauce

½ cup packed brown sugar
4 tablespoons vinegar
2 tablespoons dry mustard

Combine all ingredients and spread over ham. Baste several times while baking ham.

Bratwurst and Sauerkraut

1 (1 pound) fully cooked bratwurst
2 (15 ounce) cans sauerkraut, drained
¼ cup packed brown sugar

Cook bratwurst in a well greased skillet for 5 minutes, turning often until brown. Add sauerkraut to skillet, then sprinkle with brown sugar. Cover and cook over low heat for 10 minutes.

Baked Orange Roughy

4 orange roughy fish fillets
Melted margarine
Mrs. Dash lemon herb seasoning

Cut dark spots out of fish. Place on foil-lined cookie sheet. Brush fish with melted margarine and sprinkle with Mrs. Dash lemon herb seasoning. Bake at 400° for 5 to 8 minutes. Turn, brush other side of fish with margarine, sprinkle with seasoning and bake for 5 to 8 minutes longer or until flaky when tested with a fork.

Flounder Italiano

4 to 6 frozen, flounder fillets
1½ cups spaghetti sauce
½ cup shredded mozzarella cheese

Place fillets in a greased, 9 x 13-inch pan. Pour spaghetti sauce over fillets and bake, uncovered, at 350° for about 30 minutes. Sprinkle with cheese, then bake for 5 minutes longer or until cheese melts.

Salmon Casserole

1 (14¾ ounce) can salmon, drained, divided
1 (10¾ ounce) can cream of mushroom soup, divided
1 cup crushed potato chips, divided

Remove bone and skin from salmon. Arrange half of salmon, half of soup and half of chips in layers in a greased 8-inch baking dish. Repeat layers, ending with chips on top. Bake at 350° for 20 minutes.

Mother's Salmon Patties

1 (7½ ounce) can pink salmon, rinsed, drained
1 egg, beaten
1 cup cracker crumbs

Combine salmon, egg and crumbs; mix well. Shape into patties and fry on both sides.

Salmon Loaf

1 (14.75 ounce) can salmon, undrained
2 eggs, beaten
1 cup matzo meal

Remove bones and skin from salmon and chop. Combine salmon, eggs and meal, mixing well. Pack in a greased loaf pan. Bake at 325° for 30 minutes or until done.

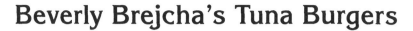

Beverly Brejcha's Tuna Burgers

1 (6 ounce) can tuna fish, drained
1 beaten egg
½ cup crushed Cheezits crackers

Combine all ingredients and mix well. Shape into patties.
Brown on both sides in a skillet that has been sprayed with
nonstick cooking spray or fry in a little vegetable oil.

Chinese Tuna Bake

2 (6 ounce) cans tuna, well drained
1 (10½ ounce) can cream of celery soup
1 (3 ounce) can Chinese fried noodles, divided

In a bowl, combine tuna, soup and half can of fried Chinese
noodles. Mix well and pour into a greased casserole dish.
Bake at 350° for 25 minutes. Remove from oven and top
with remaining noodles. Bake for 10 minutes longer.

Tuna Chip Casserole

2 cups crushed potato chips
2 (6 ounce) cans tuna fish, drained
2 (10½ ounce) cans cream of mushroom soup

Place a layer of crushed potato chips in a greased casserole
dish. Top with a layer of tuna. Repeat layers. Pour
mushroom soup over tuna and bake at 350° for 25 minutes.

Grilled Tuna Steaks

4 (6 ounce) tuna steaks
½ cup lime juice
1 clove garlic, minced

Combine lime juice and garlic in an 8 x 8-inch baking dish. Add tuna. Cover and marinate for 3 hours in the refrigerator, turning occasionally. Drain and reserve marinade. Grill over medium heat for 8 to 10 minutes on each side, basting often with the marinade.

Yield: 4 servings.

Creamed Tuna

1 (6 ounce) can tuna fish, drained
1 (10¾ ounce) can cream of mushroom soup
½ can milk

Combine all ingredients and mix well. Heat thoroughly. Serve over rice, toast, noodles or in patty shells.

Optional: Add ½ cup green peas to the creamed tuna.

Joann Lowe's Haddock Fillets

2 tablespoons lemon juice
1 tablespoon olive oil
4 haddock fillets

Mix lemon juice and olive oil together; pour into skillet and heat. Place fillets in pan and saute until brown on each side, about 5 minutes.

Bob Batterson's Fried Fish Fillets

8 fish fillets
1 cup biscuit mix or more
1 teaspoon seasoned salt

Dip fish in biscuit mix. Sprinkle with seasoned salt, then fry until golden brown on both sides. Allow 2 fillets per person.

Haddock Parmigiana

4 (4 ounce) haddock fillets, fresh or frozen
1 cup spaghetti sauce
4 mozzarella cheese slices

Place haddock in a greased baking dish. Pour spaghetti sauce over fish, covering both sides. Top each with a cheese slice. Bake at 375° for about 15 minutes or until cheese bubbles or until fish flakes easily when tested with a fork. Watch carefully.

Italian Cod Fillets

4 cod fillets
½ cup chopped onion
1 (15 ounce) can stewed tomatoes and peppers

Place cod in nonstick sprayed baking pan. Layer onions and tomatoes over fish. Bake at 350° for 30 minutes or until fish flakes when tested with a fork.

193

South of the Border Baked Cod

4 cod fillets
Thick and chunky salsa
4 slices cheddar or Monterey Jack cheese

Spray pan with a cooking spray. Place fish in pan. Spread salsa over fish and top with cheese slices. Bake at 350° until fish flakes when tested with a fork.

Fillet of Sole

4 fillets of sole
1 (10½ ounce) can cream of celery soup
Dash of paprika or lemon pepper

Lay fillets of sole in a greased, 9 x 13-inch dish. Pour soup over the fish. Bake at 350° for about 15 minutes or until fish flakes easily. Sprinkle with paprika or lemon pepper to serve.

Sole Almondine

⅓ cup slivered almonds
8 tablespoons margarine, divided
1 (2 pound) fillet of sole

Saute almonds in 4 tablespoons margarine. Add the additional margarine to almonds. Place fish in an ovenproof, glass dish. Pour almond-margarine mixture over fish. Bake uncovered at 350° for about 15 minutes or until fish flakes easily.

Sole With Yogurt-Dill Sauce

1 pound (3 ounces each) sole fillets
1 cup plain yogurt
½ teaspoon dill weed or to taste

Saute fish in a nonstick skillet that has been sprayed. Brown on both sides. Mix yogurt with dill weed to taste. Pour over fish and heat

Optional: Serve with lemon wedges.

Sole Elegante

1 (4 count) package frozen sole fillets
1 (10½ ounce) can cream of shrimp soup
½ cup grated parmesan cheese

Arrange fish in a greased baking dish. Spread soup over fish, then sprinkle parmesan cheese on top. Bake at 425° for 25 minutes.

French Fish Fillets

1 pound fish fillets
¼ cup French dressing
½ cup cracker crumbs

Dip fish in dressing and roll in crumbs coating well. Place fish in a baking dish and bake at 350º for about 10 minutes. Turn fish and cook 10 minutes longer or until fish is lightly browned.

195

Mary Alice Lawrence's Fried Catfish

Catfish
Cornmeal
Vegetable oil

Dip catfish in cornmeal and slowly fry on low heat in a little vegetable oil until golden on both sides.

Broiled Fish Fillets

⅓ cup mayonnaise
4 (5 to 7 ounce) fish fillets
3 tablespoons grated parmesan cheese

Preheat broiler. Spread mayonnaise over each fillet. Sprinkle cheese on top of each. Place in a broiler pan and broil 4 to 6 inches away from heat for 5 to 8 minutes or until fish flakes easily when tested with a fork.

Scalloped Oysters

15 saltine crackers, crushed
2 cups milk
1 pint fresh oysters

Combine cracker crumbs and milk and mix well. Stir in oysters. Pour mixture into a 9-inch greased baking pan and bake at 350° for 30 minutes.

Lobster Tails

2 tablespoons butter
1 tablespoon lemon juice
4 (8 ounce) frozen lobster tails

Microwave butter in a small bowl at high until melted. Add lemon juice to melted butter and brush mixture onto lobster meat. Face tails shell side down in baking dish. Cover with waxed paper and microwave on high for 6 to 10 minutes, turning every 3 minutes. Serve with additional melted butter, if desired.

Yield: 4 servings.

Notes

Cakes,
Candies
& Cookies

Fruit Cocktail Cake

1 box yellow cake mix
3 eggs
1 (15 ounce) can fruit cocktail, undrained

Pour all ingredients into a large bowl and mix well. Pour into a greased and floured 9 x 13-inch pan. Bake at 350° for 45 to 50 minutes.

Cream of Coconut Cake

1 (18.25 ounce) package white cake mix
1 (3½ ounce) can flaked coconut
1 (15½ ounce) can cream of coconut

Prepare cake mix according to package directions adding flaked coconut. Bake in a greased and floured 9 x 13-inch cake pan as directed. When done, remove from oven and punch deep holes in top of cake with a fork. Pour cream of coconut over cake. Cool 5 minutes.

Optional: Sprinkle with additiona coconut

Walnut Cake

1 (18.25 ounce) yellow cake mix
1 cup chopped walnuts
1 cup pancake syrup

Prepare cake according to package directions. Stir in walnuts and pour into a buttered 9 x 13-inch pan. Pour syrup over batter. Do not stir. Bake according to package directions. Serve warm.

Optional: Top with whipped cream.

Carrot Cake

1 (18.25 ounce) box spice cake mix
2 cups shredded carrots
1 cup chopped walnuts or pecans

Prepare cake mix according to package directions. Stir in carrots and nuts. Bake according to package directions in greased, floured 9 x 13-inch pan. Cool before frosting.

Frosting for Carrot Cake

1 stick margarine, softened
1 (8 ounce) package cream cheese, softened
1 (1 pound) box powdered sugar

Combine margarine and cream cheese; beat until creamy. Stir in powdered sugar and beat. Spread on carrot cake.

Quick Company Blueberry Torte

1 (21 ounce) pound cake
1 (21 ounce) can blueberry pie filling
1 (12 ounce) carton frozen whipped topping

Slice pound cake lengthwise to make 4 layers. Spread pie filling between each layer. Spread whipped topping over top and sides of cake.

Apricot Cake

1 (18.25 ounce) box lemon cake mix
3 eggs, beaten slightly
1 (15 ounce) can apricots, chopped

Combine cake mix, eggs and apricots with juice in a mixing bowl and mix well. Bake in a greased, floured 9 x 13-inch pan at 350° for 30 to 35 minutes, or until cake tests done.

Optional: While cake is warm, you may frost with a cup of apricot
jam. Cool and cut into squares.

Lemon Cheesecake

1 (8 ounce) package cream cheese, softened
1 (3.4 ounce) package instant lemon pudding mix
1 graham cracker pie crust, baked

In mixing bowl, beat cream cheese until creamy. Add pudding mix and prepare according to package directions. Pour into baked crust and chill 2 to 4 hours.

Date-Nut Spice Cake

1 (18.25 ounce) package spice cake
1 cup chopped dates
½ cup chopped pecans

Prepare cake according to package directions. Stir dates and pecans into batter. Bake in a greased, 9 x 13-inch pan as directed on box.

Optional: If you would like an icing on this cake, use Carrot Cake
Frosting on page 201.

Strawberry Shortcake

1 (21 ounce) pound cake, sliced in 12 slices
1 pint strawberries, sliced and sweetened
1 (8 ounce) container frozen whipped topping, thawed

Place 6 cake slices on 6 dessert plates. Arrange half the strawberries over the cake slices. Repeat layers. Top with whipped topping.

Strawberry Gelatin Cake

1 (18¼ ounce) package white cake mix
2 (3 ounce) boxes strawberry gelatin
1 (8 ounce) container frozen whipped topping

Make cake mix according to package directions and bake in a greased, 9 x 13-inch pan and cool. Poke holes deep in the cake with a fork. Dissolve gelatin in 1 cup boiling water. Stir in 1 cup cold water; mixing well. Let gelatin set until it reaches room temperature, then pour gelatin over the cake and refrigerate until gelatin is firm. Frost with whipped topping just before serving.

Strawberry Angel Delight

1 (3 ounce) strawberry gelatin
1 loaf-size angel food cake, cubed
2 (10 ounce) packages strawberry halves, thawed, drained

Prepare gelatin according to package directions. Cut cake into 1-inch cubes and arrange cubes in one layer in a 9 x 9-inch glass dish or bowl. When gelatin is partially jelled, stir in strawberries. Pour ½ of mixture over cake. Top with a second layer of cake cubes. Spread remaining gelatin over the top and refrigerate until firm.

Optional: You may spread 1 (8 ounce) carton frozen whipped topping over cake.

Pineapple Cake

1 (20 ounce) can crushed pineapple, drained
2 sticks margarine, sliced
1 (18.25 ounce) box white or yellow cake mix

Spread pineapple in a greased, 9 x 13-inch dish. Sprinkle dry cake mix over the fruit. Dot with slices of margarine. Bake at 350° for about 35 minutes or until browned.

Optional: A dip of vanilla ice cream gives this a special taste.

Mandarin Layer Cake

1 (18.25 ounce) box yellow cake mix
¾ cup orange juice
2 (11 ounce) cans mandarin oranges, drained, chopped

Prepare cake mix according to package directions, but add ¾ cup orange juice in place of ¾ cup of the liquid called for in the recipe. Stir in chopped oranges. Bake in 2 or 3 (8-inch) cake pans at 350° for 20 to 30 minutes. Cool and frost between layers, sides and top.

Frosting for Mandarin Orange Cake

1 (6 ounce) box instant vanilla pudding
1 (8 ounce) container frozen whipped topping, thawed
1 (20 ounce) can crushed pineapple, drained

Mix pudding and whipped topping together. Drain pineapple and fold into whipped topping and pudding mixture. Frost cooled cake.

Lemon Gelatin Cake

1 (18.25 ounce) package lemon cake mix
1 (6 ounce) package lemon gelatin
1 (12 ounce) container frozen whipped topping

Mix cake according to directions on box and bake. Remove from oven, then poke holes in top of cake. Mix gelatin, using 1 cup hot water only. When dissolved, pour gelatin over cake and allow gelatin to soak in. Let cake cool. Frost cake with whipped topping.

Christmas Fruit Cake

1 (18¼ ounce) package spice cake mix
1¼ cup candied fruit, chopped
1 cup chopped pecan

Prepare spice cake according to the directions on the box. Stir in candied fruit and pecans. Bake as directed for bundt pan.

German Chocolate Surprise

1 box German chocolate cake mix
2 cans German chocolate frosting, divided
Vanilla ice cream

Prepare cake mix as directed on package. Stir one can of German chocolate frosting into the batter. Mix well and bake as directed on cake mix package. Cool and frost with second can of frosting. Slice cake and serve each slice with a dip of vanilla ice cream.

Black Forest Cake

1 box brownie mix
1 (21 ounce) can cherry pie filling, divided
¼ cup sliced almonds

Prepare brownie mix according to package directions. Divide dough in half and spread over bottom of 2 greased, 8-inch round, baking pans. Bake at 350° for 30 minutes. Cool in pans on wire racks for 10 minutes. Remove from pans and cool completely. Place one brownie layer on a serving plate. Spoon half the cherry pie filling evenly over brownie. Place second brownie layer over filling and top with remaining cherry pie filling. Sprinkle with almonds.

Ann's Chocolate-Cherry Cake

1 (18.25 ounce) box devil's food cake mix
2 large eggs
1 (20 ounce) can cherry pie filling

Combine cake mix with 2 eggs, mixing well. Stir in cherry pie filling. Mix until well blended. Pour into a greased and floured, 9 x 13-inch pan and bake at 350° for 40 to 50 minutes. Frost as desired.

Cherries On A Cloud

1 package angel food cake mix
1 (20 ounce) can cherry pie filling
1 (8 ounce) carton frozen whipped topping

Prepare cake mix according to package directions and bake according to directions. (Use a pre-baked angel food cake from the grocery store if you need a short-cut.) Cool and slice. Place 1 slice on each dessert plate. Spoon cherries over cake. Top with whipped topping.

Apple-Spice Crisp

1 (21 ounce) can apple pie filling
1 (18.25 ounce) package spice cake mix
1 stick margarine, sliced

Spread apple pie filling in a greased, 9 x 13-inch dish. Sprinkle or spread dry spice cake mix over the fruit. Dot with slices of margarine, bake at 350° for about 35 minutes or until cake is browned.

Betty Kolbe's
Chocolate Applesauce Cake

1 (18.25 ounce) box chocolate cake mix
1 (16 ounce) can applesauce
½ to ¾ cup egg substitute or 3 eggs

Combine all ingredients in mixing bowl and blend well. Spray a 9 x 13-inch pan with nonfat cooking spray. Pour all ingredients into pan. Bake according to package directions.

Optional: If you would like icing on the cake, use 1 can prepared milk chocolate icing.

Angel Pudding Cake

1 loaf angel food cake, cubed
1 (3.9 ounce) package chocolate pudding
1 (8 ounce) container frozen whipped topping, thawed

Place cake cubes in a greased, 9 x 13-inch pan or glass dish. Prepare pudding according to package directions and spread over cake cubes. Spread whipped topping over pudding. Refrigerate 6 hours. Cut into squares to serve.

Mary Sutton's
Hawaiian Cake Frosting

1 (3.4 ounce) package instant French vanilla pudding mix
1 (20 ounce) can crushed pineapple, undrained
1 (8 ounce) carton frozen whipped topping, thawed

In a large bowl, combine pudding mix with pineapple and mix well. Fold in whipped topping. Let mixture stand for 15 minutes. Partially freeze a pound cake, then slice cake horizontally into 4 layers. Spread icing between layers and on top of pound cake. Frost cake. Refreeze cake. Slice to serve.

Children's Cake Cones

1 (9 ounce) package chocolate cake mix
1 (12 count) box ice cream cones with flat bottoms
1 (12 ounce) cake frosting of your choice

Prepare cake batter according to package directions. Pour 3 tablespoons batter into ice cream cones to fill about half full. Set cones in muffin tins and bake at 350° for 25 to 30 minutes. (These should rise to top of cone.) Cool. Frost with canned frosting.

Magic Microwave Fudge

1 (12 ounce) package semi-sweet or milk chocolate chips
1 (14 ounce) can sweetened condensed milk
1 teaspoon vanilla

Combine chocolate chips and milk in a glass dish and microwave on high for 3 minutes. Stir until melted and smooth. Mix in the vanilla. Spread evenly into a foil-lined, 8-inch, square pan and chill until firm. Cut into squares.

Optional: Add 1 cup chopped walnuts or pecans if you like nuts in your fudge.

Dick Hader's Maple Fudge

1½ cups dark corn syrup
6 cups sugar
3 (8 ounce) cartons whipping cream

Combine, mix and cook all ingredients in a large pan or skillet to soft-ball stage. Remove from heat. Beat with electric mixer until smooth and stiff. Pour onto pan and let set until firm. Cut into squares.

Louise Holtzinger's
Peanut Butter Fudge

1 (12 ounce) package chocolate chips
1 (12 ounce) jar extra chunky peanut butter
1 (14 ounce) can sweetened condensed milk

Melt chocolate chips and peanut butter together in top of a double boiler over hot water. Remove from heat and stir in milk. Pour into an 8 x 8-inch pan lined with waxed paper and let it set until firm.

Marshmallow Fudge

1 (12 ounce) package semi-sweet chocolate chips
1 (14 ounce) can sweetened condensed milk
1 (8 ounce) package miniature marshmallows

Melt chocolate chips in top of a double boiler. Remove from heat and stir until creamy. Mix in milk, then the marshmallows. Pour into a buttered pan. Cool, then refrigerate until firm. Cut into squares.

Thelma Pruitt's Strawberry Candy

2 (6 ounce) packages dry strawberry gelatin
1 (14 ounce) can sweetened condensed milk
1 (8 ounce) package flaked coconut

Combine all ingredients and mix well. Refrigerate overnight. Shape into strawberry-size balls. Refrigerate.

Optional: To really take care of your sweet tooth, roll candy in granulated sugar or crystallized sugar. There are also sugars that come in fun colors.

Chocolate-Covered Strawberries

30 whole strawberries with stems
1 (12 ounce) package chocolate chips
6 tablespoons margarine

Place clean berries on a large wax paper-lined cookie sheet. Melt chocolate chips in the top of a double boiler over hot water. Stir in margarine and mix until melted and well blended with chocolate. Dip berries in chocolate, then replace on waxed paper and refrigerate until chocolate hardens.

Chocolate-Coconut Drops

1 (8 ounce) semi-sweet chocolate
1½ cups flaked coconut
1 teaspoon almond extract

Melt chocolate in saucepan over low heat. Remove from heat, then stir in coconut and almond extract. Drop by teaspoonfuls onto waxed paper. Let set until firm or refrigerate.

Chocolate-Covered Cherries

1 (6 ounce) package chocolate chips
2 tablespoons milk
1 (8 ounce) jar maraschino cherries with stems

Melt chocolate chips in microwave or top of a double boiler. Stir in milk. Pat cherries dry and dip dry cherries into mixture and turn until coated. Lay cherries on a cookie sheet lined with waxed paper and cool until firm. The chocolate chip-milk mixture can be doubled or tripled.

Chocolate-Covered Apricots

2 ounces bittersweet chocolate
2 teaspoons shortening
24 apricot halves, fresh or dried

Melt chocolate and shortening together. Dip apricots in chocolate. Place on waxed paper on baking sheet and refrigerate until firm.

Christmas Peppermint Candy

1 (20 ounce) package white chocolate
or white almond bark
1 cup crushed peppermint sticks
1 cup toasted slivered almonds

Melt chocolate in double boiler, stirring until creamy.
Remove from heat. Stir in crushed peppermint sticks and
slivered almonds. Pour onto greased, cookie sheet and let
set until firm. Cut into squares or break into pieces. Keep in
a tightly covered container.

Pretzels-and-Peanuts
Chocolate Candy

1 pound white chocolate
3 cups pretzel sticks
1 (8 ounce) package Spanish peanuts

Melt chocolate in double boiler. Stir in pretzels and peanuts
until coated. Spread in jelly-roll pan. Let set until firm.
Break into pieces.

Peanut Clusters

1½ pounds almond bark
1 (12 ounce) package chocolate chips
1 (9 ounce) package salted peanuts

Melt 1 ½ pounds almond bark and 12 ounces chocolate chips
together in the top of a double boiler over boiling water. Stir
constantly. When melted and smooth, stir in the peanuts.
Drop by spoonfuls onto waxed paper. Let set until firm or
chill to firm.

Quick Peanut Brittle

1 cup sugar
1 teaspoon baking soda
1½ cups salted peanuts

Pour sugar in a skillet and heat on lowest setting until sugar turns a brownish color. Stir often and be careful not to burn sugar. Remove from heat. Add baking soda and mix quickly. Pour over peanuts that have been spread in a jelly-roll pan or over waxed paper.

Chinese-Noodle Candy

1 (12 ounce) package chocolate chips
1 (3 ounce) can Chinese noodles
½ cup chopped pecans

Melt chocolate in double boiler. Stir in Chinese noodles and pecans. Drop by spoonfuls onto waxed paper. Let set until they are firm.

Chocolate-Marshmallow Candy

1 pound milk chocolate
1 cup miniature marshmallows
½ cup chopped pecans

Melt chocolate in top of a double boiler. Line a 9 x 13-inch cake pan with waxed paper. Pour half of the melted chocolate over the waxed paper. Cover chocolate with marshmallows and pecans. Pour remaining half of the melted chocolate over marshmallows and pecans. Let cool completely, then break into pieces.

Lucy Wornall's Cocoa Puff Candy

1½ pounds white chocolate
4½ cups Cocoa Puffs cereal
1 (12 ounce) can red skin peanuts

Melt chocolate. Stir in cereal and peanuts. Drop by teaspoonfuls onto waxed paper. Let set until candy is firm.

Chocolate Cheerios

2 cups chocolate chips
¾ cup chunky peanut butter
3 cups plain doughnut-shaped oat cereal

Melt chocolate chips in double boiler. Mix in the peanut butter. Stir until smooth. Stir in doughnut-shaped oat cereal. Drop by spoonfuls onto waxed paper and let set until firm.

Chocolate-Butterscotch Clusters

1 (6 ounce) package chocolate chips
1 (12 ounce) package butterscotch chips
1 (12 ounce) package salted Spanish peanuts

Combine chocolate and butterscotch chips in a 2-quart, glass dish. Heat on medium power for 5 to 6 minutes or until melted. Stir after 3 minutes, then again after 5 or 6 minutes. Watch carefully for burning. (Some microwaves have a higher power.) If chips are melted before the time given here, remove immediately. Stir in peanuts and drop by teaspoonfuls onto waxed paper. Let set until firm. Store in an airtight container.

Butterscotch Flakes

1 cup butterscotch chips
½ cup peanut butter
2 or 3 cups corn flakes

Melt chips and peanut butter in a double boiler; mix well. Remove from heat and stir in corn flakes. Drop by teaspoonfuls onto waxed paper. Let set until they harden.

Candy Apples

5 red delicious apples
1 pound caramels
2 tablespoons margarine

Remove stems from apples; wash and dry. Melt caramels and margarine in top of double boiler. Stir until smooth. Push a wooden popsicle stick into each apple's stem end. Dip each apple into the caramel sauce, covering completely. Lay apples on waxed paper until they have dried and caramel has hardened.

Chocolate Leaves

Leaves
2 squares semi-sweet chocolate or ½ cup chocolate chips
1 teaspoon butter

Wash and dry 2 dozen leaves of varying sizes. Be sure they are non-poisonous leaves. Melt 2 squares chocolate and 1 teaspoon butter and mix well. Using a clean "watercolor-type" paintbrush, paint chocolate ⅛-inch thick on backs of leaves, covering well. Chill until chocolate is firm. Peel leaves off of the chocolate leaves. Decorate cakes or tarts with the chocolate leaves.

215

Peanut Butter Cookies

1 (14 ounce) can sweetened condensed milk
½ cup chunky peanut butter
½ cup chopped peanuts

Mix and drop by teaspoonfuls on greased and floured cookie sheets. Bake at 375° to 400° for 7 to 9 minutes.

Miracle Peanut Butter Cookies

1 cup chunky or extra chunky peanut butter
1 egg
1 cup sugar

Combine peanut butter, egg and sugar; mix well. Shape into balls. Flatten and crisscross with fork dipped in sugar. Bake on greased cookie sheet at 375° for 8 to 10 minutes.

Honey-Wafer Cookies

3 egg whites
½ cup honey
1 cup graham cracker crumbs

Beat egg whites until stiff. Gradually mix in ½ cup honey. Stir in graham cracker crumbs. Drop by teaspoonfuls onto well greased cookie sheets. Bake at 300° for about 8 minutes.

Forgotten Mint Puffs

3 egg whites
⅔ cup sugar
1 cup mint chocolate chips

Preheat oven to 375°. Beat egg whites to stiff peaks. Gradually add sugar, beating after each addition. Stir in mint-flavored, chocolate chips. Drop by teaspoonfuls onto greased, cookie sheet. Place puffs in oven. Turn off heat immediately. Forget puffs and leave them in the oven overnight. Do not peek inside. Puffs will be ready the next day.

Cookie Kisses

1 (18 ounce) refrigerated, chocolate chip, cookie dough
⅓ cup flour
36 chocolate kisses, unwrapped

Cut dough into 9 slices. Cut each slice into 4 pieces. Place 1 piece of dough in each greased cup of a mini-muffin pan. Press with spoon coated with flour to form cups. Place 1 chocolate kiss in each cup. Bake 10 to 12 minutes. Let cookies cool in pan 15 minutes before removing to cool on a rack.

Chocolate-Cherry Cookies

1 package chocolate cake mix
4 tablespoons cherry preserves
1 cup chocolate chips

Prepare cake mix according to package directions. Stir cherry preserves and chocolate chips into the batter. Mix until well blended. Drop by teaspoonfuls onto a greased, cookie sheet. Bake at 350° for 10 to 12 minutes or until cookies are done.

Brownie Drop Cookies

1 (19.9 ounce) package fudge brownie mix
¼ cup water
1 egg

Combine ingredients in a bowl and mix well. Dough will be stiff. Drop by teaspoonfuls onto lightly greased, baking sheet. Bake at 375° for 6 to 8 minutes. Cool slightly before removing from the cookie sheet.

Ritzy Chocolate Cookies

1 (12 ounce) jar chunky peanut butter
2 tubes Ritz crackers
1 (12 ounce) package chocolate chips

Spread a layer of peanut butter on each Ritz cracker. Melt chocolate chips in top of a double boiler over boiling water. Stir until smooth. Dip crackers in chocolate. Be sure to completely cover the peanut butter with chocolate. Lay on waxed paper to cool.

Chocolate-Coconut Cookies

2 squares chocolate
1 cup sweetened condensed milk
1 (3.5 ounce) can moist, flaked coconut

Heat together chocolate and milk; mix until smooth. Remove from heat and stir in coconut. Drop by teaspoonfuls onto a greased, cookie sheet. Bake at 350° for 8 to 10 minutes.

Forgotten Chocolate Chip Cookies

2 egg whites
⅔ cup sugar
1 cup chocolate chips

Preheat oven to 350°. Beat egg whites until frothy. Add sugar gradually and beat until stiff. Fold in chocolate chips. Drop teaspoonfuls of mixture onto greased cookie sheet. Place in oven. Turn off heat. Don't open door. Forget the cookies until the next day.

Chocolate Cookies

1 (18.25 ounce) package chocolate cake mix
½ cup oil
2 eggs, beaten

Combine all ingredients; mixing well. Drop by teaspoonfuls onto greased cookie sheets. Bake at 325° for 12 to 15 minutes.

Optional: Chopped nuts make an even better taste.

Chocolate Chip Cookies

2 cups finely crushed, graham cracker crumbs
1 cup chocolate chips
1 (14 ounce) can sweetened condensed milk

Combine all ingredients and mix well. Drop by teaspoonfuls onto a greased cookie sheet and bake at 350° for 8 to 10 minutes.

Chocolate Chip Bars

2 cups crushed graham crackers
1 cup chocolate chips
1 (14 ounce) can sweetened condensed milk

Combine and mix all ingredients. Spread in a greased 9 x 9-inch pan. Bake at 350° for 20 to 25 minutes. Cut into bars.

Gingersnaps

1 (14½ ounce) package gingerbread mix
½ cup milk
⅓ cup oil

Combine gingerbread mix, milk and oil. Beat thoroughly with an electric mixer or by hand. Drop dough by teaspoonfuls onto a greased cookie sheet about 3 inches apart. Bake at 375° for 8 to 10 minutes. Remove cookies to rack to cool.

Spice Cookies

1 box spice cake mix
2 eggs
½ cup oil

Combine and mix all ingredients. Beat until well blended. Drop teaspoonfuls of dough onto a greased, cookie sheet and bake at 325° for 8 to 10 minutes or until golden brown.

Christmas Tree Cookies

1 pound butter (not margarine)
2¼ cups powdered sugar, divided
4½ cups flour

Cream butter and add 2 cups sugar. Slowly add flour and mix until combined. Sprinkle board lightly with ¼ cup powdered sugar. Roll dough very thin, about ⅛-inch thick. Cut with Christmas tree, cookie cutters. Bake at 300° for 20 to 25 minutes.

Pecan Macaroons

2 cups finely ground pecans
2 eggs
1 cup sugar

Finely ground nuts in a blender or food processor and set aside. Beat eggs. Stir in sugar and mix well. Add pecans. Shape into balls. Place on a greased, cookie sheet. Flatten balls with a fork. Bake at 350° for 12 to 15 minutes or until lightly browned.

Chocolate Chip Macaroons

1 (14 ounce) can sweetened condensed milk
3 cups shredded coconut
½ cup chocolate chips

Combine all ingredients in a bowl and mix well. Drop by teaspoonfuls onto a greased baking sheet 2 inches apart and bake at 350° for 15 minutes. Remove from pan immediately and cool on waxed paper.

Cherry Macaroons

1 (14 ounce) can sweetened condensed milk
1 (14 ounce) package shredded coconut
½ cup candied chopped cherries

Combine and thoroughly mix all ingredients. Drop by teaspoonfuls onto greased cookie sheet and bake at 350° for about 10 minutes or until lightly browned. Cool slightly, then remove from pan.

Optional: Place extra cherry halves in middle of each macaroon before baking.

Macaroons

1 (14 ounce) package shredded coconut
1 (14 ounce) can sweetened condensed milk
1 teaspoon vanilla

Combine and mix all ingredients. Drop by spoonfuls onto a greased cookie sheet. Bake at 375° at 8 minutes. Cool before removing from pan.

Velora Holt's Marshmallow Drops

1 cup marshmallow cream
2 cups Rice Krispies cereal
½ cup raisins

Heat marshmallow cream in top of a double boiler until syrupy. Remove from heat. Pour in cereal and raisins and mix well. Drop by teaspoonfuls onto aluminum foil. Refrigerate until firm.

Optional: Use corn flakes instead of Rice Krispies for a different taste.

Chocolate-Walnut Drops

2 (1 ounce) squares unsweetened chocolate
1 (14 ounce) can sweetened condensed milk
⅔ cup chopped walnuts or pecans

Melt chocolate squares in double boiler over hot water. Stir in milk until well blended. Mix in nuts. Drop mixture by teaspoonfuls onto a greased, baking sheet. Bake at 350° for 12 to 15 minutes.

Chocolate Cherry Drops

1 (6 ounce) package chocolate chips
2 tablespoons milk
1 (8 ounce) jar maraschino cherries,
drained, patted dry, sliced

In top of double boiler over hot water, melt chocolate chips. Add milk and stir constantly to make thick sauce. Add cherries and mix well. Drop by teaspoonfuls onto waxed paper. Cool until firm.

Karen's Chocolate Peanut Butter Tarts

Butter
1 (18 ounce) roll refrigerated, ready-to-slice, peanut butter, cookie dough or chocolate chip, cookie dough
2 (13 ounce) packages Reese's bite-size peanut butter cups

Grease mini-muffin pan with butter or cooking spray. Slice cookie dough in 1-inch slices, then quarter the slices. Lay 1 piece in each mini-muffin pan. Bake at 350° for 8 minutes. While cookies are hot and puffed, gently push a peanut butter cup into the center of each cookie. Cool thoroughly before removing from tins. Keep refrigerated.

Chocolate-Pecan Brownies

1 (18.25 ounce) package brownie mix
½ cup chocolate chips
½ cup chopped pecans

Prepare brownies according to package directions. Stir in chocolate chips and pecans. Spread in a 8 x 8-inch glass, baking dish. Microwave for 7 to 8 ½ minutes on 60% power or until brownies are firm to touch. Cool. Cut into squares.

Brickle Chip Brownies

1 (18.25 ounce) box brownie mix
1 cup brickle bits
½ cup chopped pecans

Prepare brownie mix according to package directions. Stir in brickle bits and pecans. Bake according to package directions.

Chocolate-Orange Brownies

1 (15 ounce) package brownie mix
⅓ cup orange marmalade
⅓ cup chopped pecans

Prepare brownie mix according to package directions. Stir in marmalade and pecans. Bake according to package directions in a greased, floured, jelly-roll pan. Cool. Cut in 1-inch squares. (Sprinkle additional pecans over top of batter before baking, if you like.)

Low-fat Fudge Brownies

1 (19.9 ounce) box lite fudge brownie mix
1 (5.5 ounce) jar chocolate syrup
½ cup egg substitute

Combine all ingredients in a large bowl and mix until moistened. If mixture is too dry, add a little water, 1 tablespoon at a time. Spray a 9 x 13-inch glass, baking dish with non-fat cooking spray. Pour mixture into a pan and bake at 350° for 25 to 30 minutes. Cool.

Chocolate Chip Brownies

1 (15 ounce) package fudge brownie mix
1 cup chopped pecans
1 (6 ounce) package chocolate chips

Mix brownies according to package directions. Stir in pecans. Pour into a greased, floured 9 x 13-inch pan. Sprinkle with chocolate chips. Bake for 35 to 40 minutes or according to package directions. Yield: 12 to 18 servings.

Gail Ward's Graham Cracker Treats

24 graham crackers
1 cup packed brown sugar
1 cup butter or margarine

Break graham crackers into halves at perforations. Line 10 x 17-inch baking pan with foil. Arrange crackers in the prepared pan. Combine butter and brown sugar in saucepan. Heat. Boil for 2 minutes until bubbly. Spread sugar mixture over crackers. Bake at 375° for 8 minutes or until bubbly.

Optional: You may sprinkle with nuts before baking.

Butterscotch Bars

1 (12 ounce) package butterscotch morsels
1 cup chunky peanut butter
6 cups Rice Krispies cereal

Combine butterscotch chips and peanut butter in a large saucepan; stir until smooth over low heat until butterscotch morsels have melted. Remove from heat and stir in Rice Krispies. Mix until well coated. Press into a buttered, 9 x 13-inch pan. Chill until firm. Cut into squares.

Ernie Massey's Haystacks

1 cup chow mein noodles
1 cup cashews
1 (12 ounce) package butterscotch chips

Place noodles and cashews on baking sheet in single layer. Toast noodles and cashews at 250° for 15 minutes. Stir often. Melt butterscotch chips and mix with chow mein noodles and cashews. Drop in clusters by teaspoonfuls onto waxed paper and set until firm.

Chocolate Peanut Butter Cups

1 (21.5 ounce) package double-fudge brownie mix
2 eggs
2 (9 ounce) packages miniature, peanut butter cups

Preheat oven to 350°. Prepare brownie mix according to directions, using 2 eggs. Spoon into miniature, foil, cupcake liners, filling ¾ full. Place peanut butter cup in center of each and push into batter. Bake for 20 to 25 minutes or until cake tests done.

Butterscotch Krispie Bars

1 (12 ounce) package butterscotch chips
1 cup creamy peanut butter
6 cups Rice Krispies cereal

Combine butterscotch chips and peanut butter in a saucepan. Heat and stir until smooth. Remove from heat and stir in Rice Krispies cereal. Mix until well coated. Press into a buttered, 9 x 13-inch pan. Chill until firm. Cut into bars.

Lemon Bars

1 (18.25 ounce) package 1-step angel food cake mix
1 (20 ounce) can crushed pineapple, undrained
Powdered sugar

Combine dry cake mix and pineapple with juice and mix well. Pour into an ungreased, 9 x 13-inch baking pan. Bake at 350° for 30 minutes. Sprinkle powdered sugar and cut into bars.

Rice Krispies Bars

¼ cup butter or margarine
½ pound marshmallows
5 cups Rice Krispies cereal

Melt butter and marshmallows in the top of a double boiler. Stir in cereal; mixing well. Press into a buttered, 9-inch square pan and cut into bars.

227

Lucky Charm Bars

3 tablespoons margarine, melted
3½ cups miniature marshmallows
5 cups Lucky Charms cereal

Grease a 9 x 9-inch pan. Place margarine and marshmallows in a large, microwave bowl and microwave on high for 1 to 3 minutes uncovered. Stir after each minute of cooking until mixture is melted and smooth. Add cereal and mix until it is well coated. Press into pan. Let set until firm. Cut into bars.

Milky Way Squares

4 (2 ounce) Milky Way candy bars, chopped
½ cup butter or margarine
3 cups Rice Krispies cereal

Melt candy with butter and stir until blended. Stir in cereal and mix well. Pat into a greased, 11 x 7-inch pan. Refrigerate until firm. Cut into squares.

Mincemeat Squares

1⅓ cups mincemeat
1 (14 ounce) can sweetened condensed milk
2 cups graham cracker crumbs

Combine all ingredients; mixing well. Spread in a greased 9 x 13-inch pan and bake at 350° for 35 to 40 minutes. Cool before cutting into squares.

Optional: You may stir in ½ cup chopped pecans or sprinkle on top of batter before baking.

Mrs. Truman's Coconut Balls

Mrs. Truman served these at some White House gatherings.

1 (7 ounce) package shredded coconut
1 teaspoon vanilla
⅔ cup sweetened condensed milk

Combine all ingredients and mix well. Shape into balls.
Bake on greased, cookie sheets at 350° for 15 minutes

Shortbread

4 cups flour
1 cup brown sugar
1 pound butter (not margarine)

Mix flour and sugar. Cut in butter with pastry blender until
mixture is the size of green peas. Pat mixture into a rimmed,
jelly-roll pan. Bake at 325° for 40 minutes. Cut into small
squares. Turn off oven and place in oven for 10 minutes.

Gail Ward's Grandmother's Shortbread

2 cups butter
1 cup sugar
4 cups flour

Mix butter (no margarine) and all sugar until creamy.
Gradually work in flour. Mix with hands and knead 10
minutes until mixture holds together. Roll out ½-inch thick or
pat down on a breadboard. Cut into 1-inch squares. Prick
the top with a fork. Bake on ungreased cookie sheets at
275° for 45 minutes or until lightly browned.

Easy Baklava

**2 packages frozen patty shells,
thawed overnight in refrigerator
3 cups finely chopped pecans, divided
1 cup honey, warmed, divided**

Line an 8 x 8 x 2-inch cake pan with foil. Grease lightly. Set aside. Stack 3 thawed patty shells, one on top of the other. On a lightly floured surface, roll out into a 9-inch square. With a sharp knife, trim down to an 8½-inch square. Place in bottom of cake pan. Sprinkle with 1 cup pecans and drizzle with ¼ cup honey. Repeat process 3 times, making the top layer plain pastry (no nuts or honey on it). Mark pastry into diamond pattern with tip of sharp knife. Bake at 425° for 20 to 25 minutes. Cool slightly in pan. Brush surface with last of honey. Remove from pan and peel away foil. Cut into diamond shapes. Serve with more honey.

Pies & Desserts

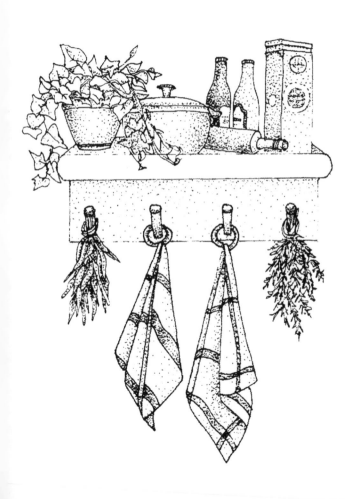

Frozen Lemonade Pie

1 (6 ounce) can frozen pink lemonade
1 (8 ounce) carton frozen whipped topping, thawed
1 (14 ounce) can sweetened, condensed milk

Combine lemonade, whipped topping and milk. Mix well; chill. Serve as pudding or pour into a graham cracker pie crust and freeze.

Key Lime Pie

1 (6 ounce) can frozen limeade concentrate
1 (8 ounce) carton frozen whipped topping, thawed
1 (14 ounce) can sweetened condensed milk

Combine all ingredients, mixing well. Pour into a prepared graham cracker crust or chocolate crumb crust. Refrigerate 2 hours or more before serving.

Coconut Cream Pie

1 (3.4 ounce) package vanilla pie filling mix
1 (7 ounce) package shredded coconut
1 (9-inch) baked pie shell

Prepare pudding as a pie according to package directions and cool. Stir in coconut. Mix well and pour into a baked, pie crust. Refrigerate for 4 hours before serving.

Optional: You may top with thawed, frozen whipped topping and sprinkle with coconut.

Chocolate-Banana Pie

1 (4.3 ounce) package cook-and-serve
chocolate pudding mix
2 to 3 bananas, sliced
1 baked pie crust

Prepare pudding according to package directions for a pie. Cool. Stir in sliced bananas. Pour into baked pie crust.

Optional: You may top with frozen whipped cream, thawed.

Speedy Banana Pie

2 to 3 bananas, sliced
1 (8-inch) baked, cooled pie crust
1 (3.4 ounce) box banana pudding

Prepare pudding as a pie according to package directions. Place banana slices in cooled crust. Pour pudding over bananas. Garnish with banana slices. Let stand 5 to 10 minutes.

Optional: For a speedy meringue, sprinkle 2 cups miniature marshmallows over top of pie and broil 2 to 3 minutes until light brown and partially melted.

Blueberry Pie A La Mode

**1 (6 ounce) 8-inch double pie crust
1 (20 ounce) can blueberry pie filling
6 to 8 scoops vanilla ice cream**

Line pie pan with 1 rolled out pie crust. Spread blueberry filling evenly in crust. Place top crust over filling and press edges together. Cut vents in it. Bake at 425° for 10 minutes. Reduce heat to 350° and bake for 25 to 35 minutes longer, or until the crust is golden brown. Cool. Slice. Place slice on dessert plate and top with dip of ice cream.

Brickle Chip Ice Cream Pie

**½ gallon vanilla ice cream, divided
1 (6 ounce) graham cracker crumb pie crust
or chocolate pie crust
1 cup brickle bits, divided**

Spoon half of vanilla ice cream into pie crust. Spread ⅔ cup brickle bits over ice cream. Top with other half of ice cream and sprinkle with remaining brickle chips. Freeze.

Optional: Serve with butterscotch sauce.

Frozen Peanut Butter Pie

**¾ cup chunky peanut butter
1 quart vanilla ice cream, softened
1 (6 ounce) graham cracker crust or chocolate crust**

Combine peanut butter and softened ice cream and mix well. Pour into pie crust and freeze.

Missouri Mud Pie

1 (8½ ounce) package chocolate wafers, divided
1 quart coffee ice cream, softened
1 jar chocolate sauce

Arrange a layer of chocolate wafers in bottom and along sides of a glass, 9-inch pie plate. Fill with ice cream. Crush additional cookies and sprinkle over the top. Freeze until firm. Slice and serve. Drizzle chocolate sauce over each slice.

Makes a 9-inch pie.

Chocolate Almond Pie

1 (8 ounce) chocolate almond bar
1 (8 ounce) carton whipped topping, thawed
1 (8-inch) graham cracker crust

Melt chocolate bar in top of a double boiler. Remove from heat and cool. Stir whipped topping into chocolate. Fill the pie crust and chill.

Optional: Garnish, if desired, by using a potato peeler to shave chocolate curls off an additional chocolate candy bar.

Chocolate Pudding or Pie Filling

1 (14 ounce) can sweetened condensed milk
3 squares semi-sweet chocolate
½ cup boiling water

Heat milk. Blend in chocolate and stir until melted. Mix in boiling water. Stir constantly until mixture thickens, about 5 minutes. Serve chilled in dessert dishes.

Optional: You may pour into a baked pie crust.

Strawberry Ice Cream Pie

1 (3 ounce) package strawberry gelatin
1 pint vanilla ice cream
1 pint fresh or frozen strawberries

Prepare gelatin with 1 cup boiling water. Mix well until gelatin is dissolved. Stir in the ice cream, then the berries. Chill and serve as pudding or pour into a prepared pie crust.

Frozen Strawberry Yogurt Pie

2 (8 ounce) cartons strawberry yogurt
1 (8 ounce) carton frozen whipped topping, thawed
1 (6 ounce) graham cracker crust or chocolate crust

Combine yogurt and whipped topping and mix. Pour into crust and freeze. Garnish with fresh strawberries, if desired.

Strawberry Pie

2 pints strawberries
3 tablespoons cornstarch
1 cup sugar

Mash 1 pint strawberries. Combine cornstarch and sugar in a saucepan. Cook on medium heat and gradually add mashed berries, stirring constantly until thickened. Cool. Pour remaining berries in a baked pie crust. Cover with strawberry-sugar mixture. Refrigerate until set.

Easy Strawberry Pie

1½ cups powdered sugar, divided
1 (9-inch) baked pie crust
1 quart fresh strawberries

Sprinkle ¼ cup powdered sugar in bottom of a pie crust. Place a layer of berries over the sugar, then sprinkle berries with more sugar. Add another layer of berries, then sprinkle with more sugar. Cover and refrigerate.

Optional: You may top with frozen whipped topping, thawed.

Cherry Cobbler

1 (20 ounce) can cherry pie filling
1 (18.25 ounce) box yellow or white cake mix
1½ sticks margarine or butter, sliced

Spread cherry pie filling in a greased 9 x 13-inch baking dish. Sprinkle with dry cake mix. Top with slices of margarine. Bake at 350° for about 35 minutes. Any pie filling or canned fruit could be substituted for the cherries.

Granny's Peach Cobbler

This recipe was given to me by my 100-year-old granny, Anna Davis of Harrison, Arkansas, who lives alone and takes care of a 4 bedroom home, cooks, makes a garden, writes songs, quilts, crochets, sews and has written and published 2 books of poetry.

1 (29 ounce) can sliced peaches with syrup
1 (18¼ ounce) package butter pecan cake mix
or yellow cake mix
½ cup melted margarine

Spread peaches in a greased 9 x 13-inch pan. Sprinkle dry cake mix over all. Drizzle margarine over cake mix. Bake at 325° for 45 to 55 minutes.

Apricot Balls

½ pound dried apricots, minced
2 cups coconut, shredded
½ (14 ounce) can sweetened condensed milk

Combine, mix and chill overnight. Shape into balls. Let set in covered container 1 day before eating.

Chocolate-Banana Crepes

4 bananas
8 crepes
½ cup chocolate syrup

Split bananas lengthwise. Lay half of 1 banana in the middle of a crepe. Fold the crepe and drizzle chocolate syrup over it.

Yield: 8 servings.

Cherry-Chocolate Bundt Cake

**1 (18.25 ounce) chocolate cake mix
1 (21 ounce) can cherry pie filling
2 large eggs, beaten**

In a bowl, combine the cake mix, pie filling and eggs; mixing well. Lightly spray a microwave bundt pan with non-stick cooking spray and pour batter in pan. Microwave on high 4 minutes. Turn bundt pan ¼ turn and microwave 4 minutes more. Turn pan ¼ turn and microwave 1 minute more on high or until cake tester comes out clean.

Yield: 12 slices.

Chocolate Ice Cream

**1 (14 ounce) can sweetened condensed milk
1 (12 ounce) container frozen whipped topping, thawed
1 gallon chocolate milk, divided**

Fold condensed milk and whipped topping into 1 quart of chocolate milk. Pour into 6-quart freezer container. Add remaining chocolate milk, then freeze according to directions.

Chocolate Syrup

**1 cup cocoa
2 cups sugar
2 cups hot water**

Mix cocoa and sugar. Add a little water to make a paste. Add remaining water and bring to a boil. Boil for 1 minute. Pour into a jar and cover with a lid. To serve as a beverage, add 1 part syrup to 4 or 5 parts milk and mix well.

Serve over frozen nonfat yogurt for a sundae or stir into a Coca-Cola for a chocolate Coke.

Fudge Sauce

Great over ice cream or over peanut butter ice cream pie.

1 cup evaporated milk
1 cup miniature marshmallows
1 cup chocolate chips

Combine Milnot, marshmallows and chocolate chips in a saucepan on medium heat until melted.

Judith's Almond Macaroons

1 (8 ounce) can almond paste
⅔ cup sugar
¼ cup egg whites (from 2-3 eggs)

In a mixing bowl, cut almond paste into small pieces. Blend with sugar. Add egg whites and beat for 4 to 5 minutes or until mixture is smooth. Drop by tablespoons onto baking sheets lined with brown paper. Leave about 1-inch space between each cookie. Bake at 350° for 18 to 20 minutes or until golden brown. Cool 5 minutes in pan. Remove from pan and cool on wire rack.

Yield: 2 dozen, half-dollar-size cookies.

Hint: If cookies stick, dampen the back of the paper with a moist cloth. After a few minutes, remove cookies from the paper.

Shaker Boiled Apples

6 red cooking apples, cored
Cold water
½ cup sugar

Place apples in a large saucepan. Add ½-inch cold water. Pour sugar over apples. Boil gently 20 minutes or until apples are tender. Turn apples over several times and stir until the sugar and water form a syrup. Serve apples with syrup in a small pitcher to pour over apples.

Yield: 6 servings.

Shaker Lemon Pie

2 lemons, thinly sliced with rind
1½ cups sugar
4 eggs

Place lemon slices in a bowl; pour sugar over them. Mix well and let stand 2 to 3 hours. Beat 4 eggs and pour over lemons. Fill an uncooked pie crust. Add a top crust. Make vents in top crust. Bake at 450° for 15 minutes. Reduce heat to 350° and bake until done.

Yield: 8 servings.

S'Mores

Graham cracker squares
Chocolate squares
Marshmallows, partially melted

Place graham cracker squares on a jelly-roll pan. Top with a square of chocolate. Lay a hot marshmallow over chocolate, then place a second cracker over marshmallow to form a sandwich.

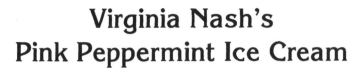

Virginia Nash's
Pink Peppermint Ice Cream

1 pound peppermint sticks, chopped
1 quart milk
1 quart cream

Drop chopped candy in milk. Cover and refrigerate overnight. Next day, pour into an ice cream freezer. Stir in cream. Freeze.

Optional: Try hard, peppermint candies instead of peppermint sticks.

Oreo Cookie Ice Cream

½ gallon vanilla ice cream, softened
1 (12 ounce) container whipped topping
2 cups crushed Oreo cookies

Mix all ingredients together and freeze in a 9 x 13-inch pan. Cut into squares to serve.

Chocolate Ice Cream Cups

1 (12 ounce) package semi-sweet chocolate chips
4 tablespoons margarine
12 scoops coffee ice cream

Combine chocolate and margarine in top of double boiler; heat until chocolate is almost melted. Remove pan from water and stir rapidly until smooth and slightly thickened. Place 12 baking cups in muffin tins. Coat inside of baking cups with chocolate. Coat thickly and evenly. Chill until chocolate is hard. Remove paper cups from chocolate by cutting around bottom edge with tip of knife, then cut up the side of the cup and pull paper away. Return shells to refrigerator until serving time. When ready to serve, fill with ice cream.

Jane Ballard's Vanilla Ice Cream

2 (14 ounce) cans sweetened condensed milk
6 cups whole milk
2 teaspoons vanilla

Combine, mix and freeze in an ice cream freezer according to freezer directions.

Makes 1½ gallons.

Chocolate Ice Cream With Raspberries

6 scoops chocolate ice cream
1 (10 ounce) package frozen raspberries in syrup
6 tablespoons chocolate syrup

Place one large scoop of ice cream in each of 4 dessert bowls. Pour ½ of the raspberries into a blender and blend until pureed. Combine with remaining ½ package berries. Pour chocolate sauce over ice cream. Drizzle raspberry mixture over all.

Nancy Reagan's Lemon Dessert

4 lemons
4 scoops lemon sherbet
Mint sprigs

Cut off bottoms of lemons so they will stand firmly on a plate. Slice ½-inch off the top. Save this cap. Scoop out lemon and juice. Fill lemon shells with lemon sherbet. Place cap of lemon back on top, plus a sprig of mint.

Orange-Pineapple Sherbet

1 (20 ounce) can crushed pineapple, undrained
1 (2 liter) bottle orange soda
2 (14 ounce) cans sweetened, condensed milk

Combine and mix all ingredients. Freeze.

Strawberry Sherbet

9 (12 ounce) cans strawberry soda
3 (14 ounce) cans sweetened condensed milk
3 (10 ounce) packages frozen sliced strawberries, thawed

Combine all ingredients; mixing well. Freeze in a 6-quart ice cream freezer.

My Grandma's
Banana Pudding Dessert

1 (3 ounce) package banana pudding
1 (12 ounce) box vanilla wafer cookies
4 to 6 bananas, sliced

Prepare banana pudding according to package directions. Make a cookie crust by placing whole vanilla wafers in bottom and along sides of a glass dish. Make layers of pudding, sliced bananas and cookies. Repeat layers until all ingredients have been used. Refrigerate 2 to 4 hours to blend flavors.

Mocha Pudding

1 (16 ounce) almond candy bar
1 tablespoon instant coffee powder
1 (12 ounce) carton frozen whipped topping

Melt candy with coffee powder in a double boiler over boiling water, mixing often. Remove from heat and cool completely. Stir in whipped topping. Serve in dessert dishes as a pudding.

Optional: You may pour into a graham cracker crust to serve as a pie. Refrigerate until firm.

Jan's Vanilla Fruit

2 (15 ounce) cans chunky fruit
1 (6 ounce) package dry instant vanilla pudding
2 bananas, sliced

(Be sure to use chunky fruit and not fruit cocktail.) Pour fruit and juice into a bowl. Add instant vanilla pudding and mix well. Stir in bananas. Spoon salad into dessert dishes. Refrigerate for 2 to 3 hours.

Optional: You may add ½ cup miniature marshmallows.

Fruit Pizza

1 (20 ounce) package refrigerated sugar cookie dough
3 cups whipped topping
2 to 3 cups assorted fresh fruit

Press dough evenly into a pizza pan and bake at 350° for 25 to 30 minutes or until golden brown. Cool completely in pan, then spread a layer of whipped topping over the crust. Arrange fresh sliced fruit of your choice over cookie pizza

Lois Davis'
Chocolate-Covered Pretzels

1 pound white almond bark
¼ teaspoon vanilla
1 (5 ounce) package pretzels,
or enough to use all of melted almond bark

Melt almond bark and stir in vanilla. Dip pretzels in melted almond bark. Place on waxed paper to dry.

Pecan-Stuffed Dates

24 pecan halves
24 pitted dates
⅓ cup powdered sugar

Stuff one pecan half in cavity of each whole pitted date. Dust powdered sugar over dates with a flour sifter.

Pears Helene

1 pint vanilla ice cream
1 (15 ounce) can pear halves, drained
½ cup chocolate sauce

Place a scoop of ice cream into 4 glass dessert dishes. Place 2 pear halves on each. Drizzle chocolate sauce over pears and ice cream.

Betty Marcason's Red Hot Apples

6 Jonathan apples
½ (9 ounce) package red hot cinnamon candies
Water

Peel and slice apples ¼ to ½-inch thick. Place in saucepan and pour red hots over apples. Add enough water to cover apples. Bring to a boil. Reduce heat, then simmer until apples are tender. Apples will turn red and have a wonderful "red hot" cinnamon taste.

Pat-In-The-Pan Pastry

1⅓ cups flour
⅓ cup vegetable oil
2 tablespoons cold water

Mix flour and oil until flour is moistened. Sprinkle 1
tablespoon of cold water at a time over mixture and toss with
a fork until all water is absorbed. Gather pastry into a ball,
then press it in bottom of pie pan and up the sides. Flute the
edges of crust and prick the bottom and sides with a fork.
Bake, unfilled, at 475° for 10 to 12 minutes. Cool. Fill with
desired pudding.

Mini Crusts

1 (3 ounce) package cream cheese, softened
½ cup margarine, softened
1 cup flour

Combine all ingredients and mix well. Chill dough. Shape
into 24 balls. Place in ungreased mini-muffin pan and press
dough against bottom and sides. Bake at 350° until golden
brown. Fill with pie filling of your choice or use to make
mini-quiche Lorraine.

Christmas Wreaths

1 stick margarine
30 large marshmallows
3 cups corn flakes

Melt margarine and marshmallows together, stirring until smooth. Remove from heat and stir in corn flakes. (Add green food coloring to make "wreath" green.) Drop by spoonfuls onto waxed paper to make a circle. Form a hole in middle with buttered fingers so these are shaped like wreaths.

Optional: Decorate, if desired, with cinnamon red hot candies dotted on each wreath.

Index

Index

Index

Index

Index

Index

Index

Index

Index

Index

Index

Index

Index

Index

263

Index

Index

Index

Index

Index

Index

Index

Index

Index

Index

Index

Index

Index

Index

Index

Index

Index

Index

COOKBOOKS PUBLISHED BY COOKBOOK RESOURCES, LLC

The Ultimate Cooking with 4 Ingredients
Easy Cooking with 5 Ingredients
The Best of Cooking with 3 Ingredients
Gourmet Cooking with 5 Ingredients
Healthy Cooking with 4 Ingredients
Diabetic Cooking with 4 Ingredients
4-Ingredient Recipes for 30-Minute Meals
Essential 3-4-5 Ingredient Recipes
The Best 1001 Short, Easy Recipes
Easy Slow-Cooker Cookbook
Essential Slow-Cooker Cooking
Quick Fixes with Cake Mixes
Casseroles to the Rescue
I Ain't On No Diet Cookbook
Kitchen Keepsakes/More Kitchen Keepsakes
Old-Fashioned Cookies
Grandmother's Cookies
Mother's Recipes
Recipe Keepsakes
Cookie Dough Secrets
Gifts for the Cookie Jar
All New Gifts for the Cookie Jar
Gifts in a Pickle Jar
Muffins In A Jar
Brownies In A Jar
Cookie Jar Magic
Easy Desserts
Bake Sale Bestsellers
Quilters' Cooking Companion
Miss Sadie's Southern Cooking
Classic Tex-Mex and Texas Cooking
Classic Southwest Cooking
The Great Canadian Cookbook
The Best of Lone Star Legacy Cookbook
Cookbook 25 Years
Pass the Plate
Texas Longhorn Cookbook
Trophy Hunters' Wild Game Cookbook
Mealtimes and Memories
Holiday Recipes
Little Taste of Texas
Little Taste of Texas II
Texas Peppers
Southwest Sizzler
Southwest Olé
Class Treats
Leaving Home
Easy One-Dish Meals

cookbook
≈*resources*® LLC

To Order: *The Best of Cooking with 3 Ingredients*

Please send_____ hardcover copies @ $19.95 (U.S.) each $ _____

Texas residents add sales tax @ $1.65 each $ _____

Please send_____ paperback copies @ $16.95 (U.S.) each $ _____

Texas residents add sales tax @ $1.40 each $ _____

Plus postage/handling @ $6.00 (1st copy) $ _____

$1.00 (each additional copy) $ _____

Check or Credit Card (Canada-credit card only) Total $ _____

Charge to: ❑ MasterCard.   or   ❑ VISA

	Mail or Call:
Account # _____	Cookbook Resources
	541 Doubletree Dr.
Expiration Date _____	Highland Village, Texas 75077
	Toll Free (866) 229-2665
Signature_____	(972) 317-6404 Fax

Name _____

Address_____

City_____State_____Zip_____

Telephone (Day)_____(Evening)_____

To Order: *The Best of Cooking with 3 Ingredients*

Please send_____ hardcover copies @ $19.95 (U.S.) each $ _____

Texas residents add sales tax @ $1.65 each $ _____

Please send_____ paperback copies @ $16.95 (U.S.) each $ _____

Texas residents add sales tax @ $1.40 each $ _____

Plus postage/handling @ $6.00 (1st copy) $ _____

$1.00 (each additional copy) $ _____

Check or Credit Card (Canada-credit card only) Total $ _____

Charge to: ❑ MasterCard.   or   ❑ VISA

	Mail or Call:
Account # _____	Cookbook Resources
	541 Doubletree Dr.
Expiration Date _____	Highland Village, Texas 75077
	Toll Free (866) 229-2665
Signature_____	(972) 317-6404 Fax

Name _____

Address_____

City_____State_____Zip_____

Telephone (Day)_____(Evening)_____